The Student's Guide
to Writing

Macmillan Study Guides

How to Begin Studying English Literature (second edition)   *Nicholas Marsh*
How to Study a Jane Austen Novel (second edition)   *Vivien Jones*
How to Study Chaucer (second edition)   *Robert Pope*
How to Study a Joseph Conrad Novel   *Brian Spittles*
How to Study a Charles Dickens Novel   *Keith Selby*
How to Study Foreign Languages   *Marilyn Lewis*
How to Study an E. M. Forster Novel   *Nigel Messenger*
How to Study a Thomas Hardy Novel   *John Peck*
How to Study a D. H. Lawrence Novel   *Nigel Messenger*
How to Study James Joyce   *John Blades*
How to Study Linguistics   *Geoffrey Finch*
How to Study Milton   *David Kearns*
How to Study Modern Drama   *Kenneth Pickering*
How to Study Modern Poetry (second edition)   *John Peck*
How to Study a Poet (second edition)   *John Peck*
How to Study a Renaissance Play   *Chris Coles*
How to Study Romantic Poetry   *Paul O'Flinn*
How to Study a Shakespeare Play (second edition)   *John Peck and Martin Coyle*
How to Study Television   *Keith Selby and Ron Cowdery*
Linguistic Terms and Concepts   *Geoffrey Finch*
Literary Terms and Criticism (second edition)   *John Peck and Martin Coyle*
Practical Criticism   *John Peck and Martin Coyle*
Studying History   *Jeremy Black and Don M. MacRaild*
The Study Skills Handbook   *Stella Cottrell*

The Student's Guide to Writing

Grammar, Punctuation and Spelling

John Peck and Martin Coyle

MACMILLAN

First published 1999 by
MACMILLAN PRESS LTD
Houndmills, Basingstoke, Hampshire RG21 6XS
and London.
Companies and representatives
throughout the world.

ISBN 0–333–72742–8

A catalogue record for this book is available
from the British Library.

This book is printed on paper suitable for recycling and
made from fully managed and sustained forest sources.

10 9 8 7 6 5 4 3 2 1
08 07 06 05 04 03 02 01 00 99

Typeset by Forewords, Oxford/Longworth Editorial Services
Longworth, Oxfordshire.

Printed in Malaysia

Contents

About this Book

This book tackles the problem of writing – how to do it, how to get things right and how to avoid the kind of simple errors that can lose marks in an essay or examination. The audience we are primarily writing for is students: we are concerned with the question of how each and every student, and especially the university student, can become a better writer. The advice the book contains, however, should prove useful to anyone who has to write on a regular basis, be it at school, in college, at work or merely on a social basis. We are concerned to help all students to communicate better and to gain confidence in their writing abilities.

Our experience is that most books about how to write don't actually help that much. Where most of them go wrong is that they offer a comprehensive guide to grammar, usually overwhelming the reader with information. They don't really confront the problem that the difficulty most people have is how to write effective and coherent sentences; they don't really consider that points about grammar or punctuation only make sense in the context of the need to write. The principle we have adopted in this book, therefore, is that knowing the definition of grammatical terms is far less important than being able to write clearly. The book does contain points about grammar, but these are secondary to the stress we put on the importance of learning how to write.

We have, consequently, deliberately limited the advice we offer to three key areas: how to write a sentence, how to punctuate and how to use words correctly (an area that includes spelling). It may be that you are particularly concerned about just one of these areas and will want to focus on the chapters dealing with that; for example, you may want to concentrate specifically on the chapters on sentences and essay-writing (chapters 1, 4 and 7), or on punctuation (chapters 2, 5 and 8), or on spelling (chapters 3, 6 and 9). It is, however, important to see how these three aspects of writing go together and complement one another: you cannot expect to write well if you neglect spelling or punctuation. For this reason we decided against dividing the book into three separate writing, punctuation and spelling sections, and have instead put the emphasis on how to move from writing correctly to how to write with confidence, and then how to write with style. Inevitably along the way there are things to be learnt – we have included lists of commonly misspelt words and words frequently confused – but we have tried to put these into a context where they will be seen as necessary skills.

If you can master the basic skills of how to write a sentence, punctuate it and present it accurately, there is no limit to how good a writer you can become. But you must make sure that you are in total command of these basic – and essential – skills. There is, however, as we have suggested above, a further dimension to writing. Basic correctness is vital, but most of us also want to sound intelligent, mature, sophisticated, even witty, when we write. We deal with such matters as the book progresses. Everything starts, though, with your ability to write a grammatical sentence, which is where the first chapter starts.

We ought to admit that there are limitations to this book that we are aware of. Neither of us pretends to be expert on modern linguistics or anything other than very basic grammar. If you are interested in these topics, then you need to consult other books recommended by your teachers. The field of language studies is constantly changing just as language itself is constantly being changed by speakers and writers. Some of the advice we offer, therefore, may strike a number of people as old-fashioned or illiberal, but we take the view that what students need to know is how to employ and make sense of the established conventions of formal writing. Once they know these, they have access to those areas of life where the written word is extremely powerful, areas such as the law, publishing and government. They can also then choose whether or not to break the traditional 'rules'; for example, by starting sentences with 'And' or 'But'. Not to know the conventions, however prescriptive these may seem, leaves students in the dark.

We are, then, interested in helping students to gain access to the shared conventions of formal, standard English. Although we talk about what is 'correct' or 'right', our intention is to show students how to reproduce those conventions which matter because they lead both to education and employment. They matter, that is, precisely because they are the conventions of those who make decisions and influence the lives of the rest of us. They are, in a sense, as basic as knowing not to turn up to an interview with dirty shoes and torn clothes. They are not absolute conventions given by God. They are, however, different from the conventions that operate in speech or in creative writing or in many other forms of communication.

They are different, but not better. We are not seeking in this book to deni-grate other forms of writing or speech or dialects or accents. Our concern is with what is appropriate to formal writing.

Our own style is deliberately informal, often breaking some of the 'rules' we mention. Part of the reason for this lies in the problem of how to make a book about spelling, punctuation and grammar both relevant and interesting. We have tried to direct the book towards the problems we have come across and to recommend solutions which we think have helped our students. We do not expect everyone to agree with the advice we offer, and, indeed, we are extremely grateful to those readers of the draft of the book who challenged and chastised us about some of the points we make. There are, we know, still areas of the text that they will not approve of, but the real test of the book will be whether students find it useful in solving their writing problems. In this context, we are extremely grateful to the following students at Cardiff University who read and commented upon the typescript of this book: Abigail Ash, Amanda Corbett, Rachel Douglass, Rhiannon Leyshon, Sophie Morrison, Kesner Ridge, Johanna Taylor and Julie Theivendran.

As we have indicated above, the structure of the book is unusual in that we deal with a limited number of topics and then circle back to them to add a little more detail. In some cases we repeat a point from an earlier chapter in order to ensure it is not forgotten. We hope that this structure enables readers to feel they are making progress and that chapters do not add too much in the way of another layer of new information or points to be grasped. We have, for the most part, excluded exercises and activities in the book: reading the book is itself a kind of exercise, where we ask you to recall a point or to move forward having absorbed previous chapters. We have, though, included at the end a note on grammar and a brief summary of twenty key points. Our primary aim, however, is to encourage you to take a fresh and considered look at how you write.

John Peck and Martin Coyle
Cardiff University

Part One
Writing Correctly

1 Writing a Sentence

Points covered
- ▶ Producing 'correct' sentences
- ▶ How sentences go wrong
- ▶ Constructing 'complex' sentences
- ▶ Summary

This is the chapter you are most likely to skip. The fact that you have bought or borrowed this book shows that you want to improve your writing skills, but the likelihood is that you are looking for advice on how to fine-tune your performance or perhaps for a 'quick-fix' solution to a problem. The chances are that you do not want to waste your time reading about something as elementary as 'a sentence'. Our experience as teachers in a university, however, where students might be expected to be competent writers, has shown us that the most common weakness in students' writing is the inability to generate sentences that are not only readable and understandable but also grammatically correct in a conventional, formal sense. This is not a new problem; people have always had difficulties handling the basic mechanics of sentences. Part of the reason for this may lie in the sort of technical vocabulary sometimes used to explain the mechanics of language which can be off-putting, although the number of technical terms you actually need to know is very small. The good news, however, is that once the basics of sentence construction are grasped, everything else will fall into place. This is because the sentence is the basis of essay-writing. Indeed, the main thing students need to know is how to construct grammatical sentences. Fortunately, this is a skill that is easy to acquire. Please, therefore, do not skip this chapter. On the contrary, if you are only going to read one chapter of this book, make sure it is this one.

▶ Producing 'correct' sentences

The essential skill in writing is the ability to generate a 'correct' sentence, followed by another 'correct' sentence, and so on. By 'correct' here we mean a sentence that follows the conventions of standard English in terms of punctuation, spelling and grammar. The eventual advantage, from the student point-of-view, of being able to do this is that employers value anyone who can write grammatical sentences and convey information clearly and accurately. Think about it: if you receive a letter that includes a sentence such as *Student's, insuring there property, a top priority for this coming year*, you might have doubts about the reliability of the firm. Your doubts would probably grow if the next sentence continued: *We offer a service, that is hard to beat and at a price, thats hard to beat for under-graduates*. If you can see that there are mistakes here, you have stood back from the sentences and read them critically and knowingly as a user of the language. You must try to develop a similar detached response to your own writing; repeatedly, and automatically, you should stand back just a little from your work and reflect on whether what you have said makes good sense. In order for any sentence to communicate effectively, it must follow some basic rules.

This is, however, only true of written sentences. Perhaps the most important thing to realise about using language is that speaking and writing are very different activities with different conventions that we need to keep separate. In speech we rattle along, communicating in a highly effective but usually less precise and less formal manner than in writing. We make endless adjustments, often repeating ourselves and rephrasing what we have said, in order to make sure that the person listening understands us. Our body language and our facial expressions all aid this process. As most of us know from foreign holidays, it is even possible for two people who do not speak the same language to conduct a 'conversation'. This is one of the advantages of spoken language, that it lends itself readily to situations and seems infinitely flexible. The same is true of written language, though on a lesser scale: we can use it creatively and informally, as, for example, in advertising or in e-mail or in different forms of writing such as journals and diaries. In this book, however, as we have noted in the introduction, we are concerned with the formal aspects of writing: with the production of essays for academic and professional purposes. These are very different kinds of activity from the informal ones or speech and need to be kept separate so as to avoid confusion.

In formal writing, every sentence has to be grammatically cohesive in order to be clear and comprehensible; it has to hang together as a unit. In this chapter we concentrate on the task of achieving this level of basic correctness (in chapters 4 and 7 we return to the subject, looking at some of the other issues involved in composing an effective sentence). Our main advice, as it will be throughout this book, is this: keep it simple and you will not go wrong. It is a far better idea to produce writing that is clear and correct than something that is ambitious but faulty. Your real target, however, is to produce work that is straightforward and methodical in structure, yet complex in terms of the ideas expressed; if you can write correct sentences you will be able to achieve this goal.

'Simple' sentences

We want to start with simple sentences:

> My grandfather likes football.

> My sister has red hair.

> I collect stamps.

A sentence is a grammatically complete unit, a group of words that makes sense. These are simple sentences, and the technical term for them is also 'simple' sentences. They consist of a **subject**, a **verb** and an **object**. In the first example, *My grandfather* is the subject, *likes* is the verb and *football* is the object. Usually the subject comes first in the sentence: it is what the sentence is about. Traditional grammars speak of the subject as the 'doer of the action', and this can be a useful way of remembering what a subject is. Then follows the verb which '**agrees**' with the subject, the two going together: we write *He likes* but *I like*. The verb must match the subject; we all recognise *I likes* as a deliberate breaking of this rule, perhaps acceptable in speech but never in formal writing. The object, if there is one in the sentence, usually follows the verb.

Every sentence needs at least a subject and a **finite verb**: for example, *David coughed*. Finite means that the verb shows when something was done, that it has a tense. So, *David coughs* is the present tense; *David coughed* is the past tense. Most people would know that if we wrote *David coughing* that something was wrong with the sentence, that we would need to insert another verb part such as *is* or *was*. And most people would realise that we cannot write *David to cough* and make sense. For sentences to work, they have to have the appropriate verb form, and this is usually the present or the past tense, or a combination of words using additional verbs such as *will*, *shall*, *could*, *is*. The only exception is sentences such as *Help*, where the subject and object are implicit. *Help*, as such, is really a condensation of something like 'Please will you help me?', but that might be a bit of a mouthful to shout if you were drowning.

Subject–verb–object

The commonest structure of simple sentences is, then, subject–verb–object:

Subject	Verb	Object
My grandfather	likes	football
My sister	has	red hair
I	collect	stamps

Can you see from these examples how straightforward the logic of a sentence is? You have a subject, and then you go on to offer a little more information about the subject through the verb and the rest of the sentence.

The subject names something; the verb is what the subject does or is. Whenever you write you should be making a quick mental check that your sentences have a subject, verb and, usually, an object. Making such a check should become instinctive, just as we instinctively check various things when driving. But even the most confident writers need now and then to stop and make a precise check of their sentences. Sometimes the subject, verb and object might take a moment to find. Look, for example, at this sentence:

In May 1997, Britain changed direction when Tony Blair won a landslide victory.

There seem to be several subjects and verbs in this sentence. The same is going to appear to be the case in nearly all sentences that consist of more than a few words. The fact is, however, that most of the words in this sentence are merely supporting the main subject and verb: **Britain changed direction**. The presence of the subject and verb is most easily revealed by asking which words could be omitted and the sentence still make sense: **In May 1997** is just a phrase telling us when something happened; **when Tony Blair won a landslide victory** has a subject (**Tony Blair**) and a verb (**won**) and an object (**a landslide victory**), but this is not what the sentence is about, its main topic. Of the three groups of words, only **Britain changed direction** can stand on its own as a sentence.

The above discussion has taken us a long way towards getting hold of sentences. It is worth remembering, however, that underlying the whole business is the simple sentence of the kind we are taught in primary school. One of the first things we learn is how to write simple sentences: **Janet likes John.** Sometimes, however, we forget the vital things we learnt years ago and also undervalue them. They are useful because they reinforce the basics. A sentence starts with a capital letter, and finishes with a full stop or a question mark or, very rarely, an exclamation mark. It has a subject and a main verb. At primary school you might be expected to write something along the following lines:

> My name is Charlotte. I am six. I collect stickers. I have two brothers. I am going to be an airline pilot.

It might seem like labouring the point, but try to see how there is a subject and verb, or subject–verb–object pattern in each of these sentences. Don't be put off by the fact that in the last sentence the verb consists of more than one word – *am going to be*. Similarly, the subject in a sentence can be more than one word. If Charlotte had decided to complete her self-portrait with the comment that *Life sucks*, we would probably be surprised, but we might also note that she has constructed a perfectly sound subject (*Life*) and verb (*sucks*) sentence.

One issue we have ducked so far is what to do about sentences that do not have an object, as in *My name is Charlotte*, *I am six*, *I am going to be an airline pilot*, or:

> My mum is a civil servant.

> My dad plays in a band.

We should be able to see that *My mum* is the subject, and *is* the verb. What, though, of the other words in the sentence, *a civil servant*? What should we call them? They are clearly not the object: *My mum* does not do anything to *a civil servant*. The term linguists use for these other sentence elements is **complement**, whereas the words in the second example *in a band* are called an **adverbial**, but the important point is to recognise that they are not the object in the sentence. Sentences do not need an object, but they do need a subject and a verb.

Here we want to take stock and repeat the key points. There are a lot of terms used to describe and analyse the structure of sentences, but the only ones you really need to know are **subject**, **finite verb** and **object**. For all other practical purposes you can label everything else 'other sentence elements'. We will, inevitably, be using other terms below, but you would be surprised just how many students suddenly find they can sort out their writing problems once they know these three basic terms and see how they underpin all sentences.

Compound sentences

Writing would, of course, be easy if it consisted exclusively of the generation and proliferation of simple sentences like those above. But it would also become boring and repetitive, and impose limits on what we could say, what ideas we could express (*My name is Hamlet. I live in Denmark. I want to be. I do not want to be.*). Imagine a history essay constructed exclusively from simple sentences:

> Adolf Hitler was born in 1889. He was born in Austria. He worked as a house-painter. He fought in the First World War. He became leader of the National Socialist Party. He became Chancellor of Germany. The Second World War started in 1939. Hitler was Germany's leader. He was a dictator. He killed millions of Jews. He died in 1945. The war ended in 1945.

Somewhere along the way, between starting and leaving school, we acquire the ability (or should acquire the ability) to add variety and interest to such a simple sequence of sentences. We add more information, and probably ideas, to complement the basic facts, but our work will also start to sound more thoughtful as we develop and change the structure of the sentences. It is also the case that a long sequence of simple sentences is difficult for the reader to follow since there seem to be no connections between the points. By the time of GCSE, however, the information above might appear as follows:

> Adolf Hitler was born in Austria, in 1889. He worked as a house-painter and fought in the First World War, subsequently becoming leader of the National Socialist Party and Chancellor of Germany. Hitler was then Germany's leader during the Second World War, which started in 1939; he was a dictator, and responsible for the death of millions of Jews. He died at the conclusion of the war, in 1945.

There is nothing essentially new or different about this account, as compared to the first version, but it has become more readable as opposed to the previous listing of the facts. What has changed? In what way have the sentences become more complicated in structure and, consequently, more weighty in tone?

The first complication consists simply of bringing two facts together in one sentence: the date of Hitler's birth is added as a phrase or element after the details of his place of birth. But the structure we want to focus on initially is the 'double (or compound) sentence': *He worked as a house-painter and fought in the First World War*. The connecting word in a compound sentence is likely to be either 'and', 'but' or 'or'. A compound sentence is as straightforward as this: it is two simple sentences joined by a connecting word. We should say that the result of joining the two sentences is a multiple sentence, that is a sentence with more than one clause. The term **clause** is just another way of describing the basic elements of subject, verb and object in a sentence. So, in a compound sentence such as the one above you get two main clauses: *He worked as a house-painter*, and then a second clause *fought in the First World War*. Each of these has a subject (*He*) and each of them a finite verb (*worked*, *fought*). They are main clauses because each of them could stand on its own as a sentence and make sense.

Compound sentences, then, are basically just simple sentences joined together by a conjunction. You can have more than two clauses, but the key thing to remember is the conjunction: *She worked as a sculptor and wrote novels and designed buildings and then became an MP*. This is very heavy-handed and illustrates why we usually combine just two simple sentences at a time. It would be more stylish to write: *She worked as a sculptor, wrote novels, designed buildings and then became an MP*. Notice the 'and' joining the last part of the sentence to the rest. Although the compound sentence is a very straightforward structure, it can be used, as this last example shows, to produce a strong impact.

'Complex' sentences

We have, however, put together a more complicated sentence than this in the passage above:

> He worked as a house-painter and fought in the First World War, subsequently becoming leader of the National Socialist Party and Chancellor of Germany.

Just as a simple sentence becomes jerky and monotonous, it is almost equally monotonous to have too many main clauses that depend upon a linking 'and'. In this case, therefore, we have added a comma after *War* and then created a **subordinate or dependent clause**. As its name suggests, this is a clause that depends on the main clause and cannot stand on its own as a sentence: *subsequently becoming leader of the National Socialist Party and Chancellor of Germany* is not a sentence. Most subordinate clauses are introduced by words such as 'although', 'because', 'if', 'when', 'until', 'unless'. The purpose of subordinate clauses is to add something extra to the main statement contained in the main clause or clauses. Complex sentences are so-called because their structure is more complex than that of simple sentences, not because they contain more complex ideas.

Nevertheless, because complex sentences display a more sophisticated sentence structure, they immediately add a feeling of maturity of expression to the sentence. This kind of use of a subordinate clause is the main complication to get hold of in sentence construction; if you can use subordinate clauses confidently, you can say anything. But if you can consciously vary the kind of sentences you write, changing perhaps from simple to compound to complex, or by deliberately using a simple sentence structure for dramatic effect, then you will also show your reader that you are in control of your material and have thought about both its form and content.

We expand on subordinate clauses in the last section of this chapter, but before we proceed any further we want to make sure that you have thoroughly absorbed the basic rules. To recap: a sentence must have a subject and a verb. Sometimes the subject and verb will be supported by additional words and clauses, but at the heart of most sentences are the subject, a verb and an object. If you have a subject, a verb and an object, then the sentence can be assumed to be working properly as a sentence. All too often, however, as we consider in the next section, students make grammatical mistakes in putting sentences together.

▶ How sentences go wrong

Most sentences that go wrong, go wrong in the same ways. They fail to comply with the rules about sentence structure. It is, of course, true that we can get in a tangle when we construct an elaborate sentence to make a complicated point, but this kind of snarled-up sentence is a far less common problem than sentences that fall apart because they fail to follow the elementary rules. There are two main mistakes that all writers of English make. They either produce would-be sentences that are not sentences but merely fragments; or they produce would-be sentences that are not sentences but two or more sentences run together: sometimes a comma is used to link the two sentences, and sometimes the two sentences are simply fused together. It is easy to make these mistakes, especially when drafting work, but it also very easy to correct them.

Sentence fragments
Both 'fragments' and 'running-together' stem from not recognising the

difference between writing and speech, a point we have touched on before. We use both 'fragments' and 'running together' over and over again when we are speaking. By 'fragments' we mean incomplete sentences: they are fragments because they cannot stand alone and make grammatical sense even though they are presented as sentences, and even though we know what they mean. Look at these examples:

The behaviour of members of parliament has been widely criticised. *Which isn't surprising*.

Algernon Ponsonby-Smythe's appearance seems to sum him up. *A chinless wonder*.

Lottery winners have lots of money and very little to do all day. *Unlike the majority of people*.

In each case, the last few words in italics after the main sentence pretend to be a sentence but they are not. They are fragments: they lack a subject and they lack a finite verb. There are two ways of correcting the 'fragment' mistake. The additional phrase could either be absorbed into or added to the sentence that precedes it, or it could be rewritten as a complete and self-sufficient sentence. We could reconstruct the last example, therefore, either as:

Lottery winners have lots of money and very little to do all day, unlike the majority of people.

Or as:

Lottery winners, unlike the majority of people, have lots of money and very little to do all day.

Or as:

Lottery winners have lots of money and very little to do all day. This is quite unlike the majority of people.

In the first instance, a comma is substituted for the full stop. In the second instance, the fragment has been absorbed into the main frame of the sentence. In the third instance, the addition of a subject (**This**) and a verb (**is**) has turned the phrase into a main or independent clause so that it can stand on its own as a second sentence.

Fragments often appear in examination essays, particularly when the candidate is telling a story or describing a sequence of events or actions:

David Copperfield moved to London. *Where he met Micawber*.

Napoleon returned as the leader of the French. *Until the Battle of Waterloo was over*.

The chemical mixture gave off a pungent smell. *While the colour remained the same*.

There are different ways of correcting these; for example:

David Copperfield moved to London, where he met Micawber.

Napoleon returned as the leader of the French until the Battle of Waterloo was over.

The chemical mixture gave off a pungent smell, while the colour remained the same.

In each of these cases, the fragment at the end is, in fact, a subordinate clause that cannot stand on its own. Subordinate clauses are parts of sentences, that amplify or modify the meaning of what has gone before, rather than complete sentences. They depend for their sense on the main sentence before them. You should try to avoid such fragments. They are not only grammatically incorrect from a formal point of view, but they also make your work seem disjointed. They create the impression that you are thinking in little steps rather than seeing, and writing about, an issue as a whole. In that respect, they do not communicate your ideas very effectively to your reader. In addition, they create a chatty tone that is inappropriate in the formal context of an essay.

Comma splices

People who litter their work with fragments are equally likely to resort to 'run-together' sentences. Look at this example:

I went down the pub with my friends, when I got home I discovered I'd lost my wallet, along with all my credit cards, even though I wanted to go to bed, I had to start making phone calls to get my cards cancelled, however, they turned up later.

If this were speech, it would be perfectly acceptable (though hard to say without obvious pauses): an everyday experience conveyed in everyday language. It is, however, totally unsatisfactory as a written account. It might make sense in this instance, but the structure is monotonous, and there would be problems if the person wanted to convey an idea rather than just a sense of what happened next. What is wrong here is that a comma is being used repeatedly as the only device to keep the long sentence under control. The term for this is a 'comma splice', meaning that clauses are joined by a comma when they should be divided into sentences or joined by conjunctions or punctuated differently. A corrected version of this example might read as follows:

> I went down the pub with my friends. When I got home I discovered I'd lost my wallet, along with all my credit cards. Even though I wanted to go to bed, I had to start making phone calls to get my cards cancelled. However, they turned up later.

Sometimes sentences are run together without even the use of a comma. In these cases we can refer to the sentences as being fused – for example: *I heard him sing it was awful*. Here we have three possible ways of putting things right: *I heard him sing; it was awful*; *I heard him sing. It was awful*; *I heard him sing, and it was awful*. All three ways separate the original fused sentence into its two clear parts.

Comma-splicing and fusing can take the form seen in the examples above, where we have exaggerated to make the point, but far more common as a mistake in student essays is an occasional breach of the rules, where the writer forgets and combines two quite separate sentences. Consider this example:

> Water is the most important compound on earth, it is found on the surface and in the atmosphere. It is also present in animals and plants.

The comma here is a comma splice. There are actually three main sentences:

> Water is the most important compound on earth. It is found on the surface and in the atmosphere. It is also present in animals and plants.

These are three simple sentences using the same format. The writer tried in the first version to avoid this, but as a result ended up splicing two sentences together. A way round this might have been: *Water, the most important compound on earth, is found on the surface and in the atmosphere*.

Here is a typical example of a fused sentence:

> She did really well at school she came top of the class again this year.

The clue to the fusing is the repetition of the word 'she'. Notice that to make sense of this sentence as it stands we have to pause after *school*. There are, in fact, two sentences here:

> She did really well at school. She came top of the class again this year.

Alternatively, we could use a subordinate clause structure:

She did really well at school, coming top of the class again this year.

It is, of course, quite possible that you might look at these last few examples and wonder whether any of this matters. You might feel that the 'unconventional' version is just as clear as the 'conventional ' version of the sentence. And perhaps it is in an isolated, simple sentence. Unless you maintain control over all the basic structures such as these, however, your written work is going to get in an awful tangle as you attempt to say more and to write at greater length. In particular, you will find you cannot handle the expression of a complex idea in your written work if the sentence collapses in the very process of trying to formulate the idea. More importantly, if you rely upon fragments, comma-splicing and fused sentences, you will create an impression that you are a less than competent writer. By contrast, if you show that you are in charge of your writing and know the appropriate conventions, you will create a positive impression of someone with something to say worth reading.

▶ Constructing 'complex' sentences

So far we have focused on constructing relatively simple sentences and avoiding the most common errors. As a student, however, you will want to progress far beyond this. You will want to ensure that you write in an effective and clear way, but also that you interest your reader and persuade them of the worth of your ideas. A useful resource for this are **complex sentences**. This, as we indicated above, is a technical term, meaning a sentence made up of one independent main clause and one or more dependent (that is, subordinate) clauses. Here is a 'complex' sentence:

Even though it is an expensive place to live, London remains a great lure.

This, obviously, is a sentence about London. It begins with a subordinate clause: *Even though it is an expensive place to live*. There then follows the main clause: *London remains a great lure*. Notice that the main clause could stand on its own as a sentence, but the subordinate clause could not. We could, of course, turn the whole sentence round and begin with the main clause and then add on the subordinate clause: *London remains a great lure, even though it is an expensive place to live*.

As we noted earlier, the reason for incorporating subordinate clauses into your work is that they enable you to put together sentences that convey more information, more ideas, and more nuances of thought and expression. Consider this passage:

> Although we know nothing for certain about the origin of the universe, we can surmise that it began with an explosion. The most recent evidence for this comes from the work of astronomers, though it has yet to be measured against other theories. While it may turn out to be just another theory, its importance could be that it leads eventually towards a new understanding of the earth's position in the solar system and, if we are to believe the reports, a new grasp of the significance of sun-spots.

As you can see, the structure of the sentences has to be fairly intricate to control and express the range of ideas. But it is a two-way street. The structure of the sentences has to be disciplined, conforming to the established grammatical rules for constructing a sentence, in order to impose control over ideas that, otherwise, might evade clear definition.

What we also have to recognise, of course, is that it is at this stage that many people start to have real problems with their written English. It is all very well writing down simple ideas in simple sentences, but in venturing further things can start to fall apart. The transition, however, is worthwhile: if you can construct and control complex sentences, you will find you can manage any writing task you are set.

Subordinate clauses

We have encountered two main problems with the work of university students. First, as we have suggested above, there are students who produce work in which the sentences are almost invariably a little too simple, and this creates an overall impression of conceptual simplicity. The effect is of a string of points, as if the writer expects the reader to forge the connections between them. The second problem we regularly encounter, however, is just the opposite: students who, because they are trying to say complicated things, run into difficulty in framing sentences to express their thoughts. Where both groups of students go wrong is that they fail to see how the basic rules of constructing sentences, if followed with a degree of self-awareness, can enable more intricate ideas to be expressed in a very controlled and confident way. The main thing that is involved here is being aware of the logic of how to position and introduce a subordinate clause. In order to illustrate this, we want to return to the information we used earlier about Hitler. At that stage we illustrated simple sentences and compound sentences, and began to touch on subordinate clauses. If we return to that material, we can produce another version of it:

Adolf Hitler, who was born in Austria in 1889, worked as a house-painter and fought in the First World War before becoming the leader of the Nationalist Socialist Party and, subsequently, the Chancellor of Germany.

Through the use of two subordinate clauses (*who was born in Austria in 1889* and *before becoming the leader of the Nationalist Socialist Party and, subsequently, the Chancellor of Germany*), several sentences have been compressed into a single sentence, but it is still easy to follow as the sentence is disciplined and obeys grammatical rules. The main benefit for the student, however, is that the compression makes the sentence seem more considered and weighty than the same ideas expressed in a sequence of simple sentences. The reader can grasp and think about the related points but also see that the writer has thought about the way to present the material.

One advantage, then, of the complex sentence is that it introduces an extra degree of polished construction into your work. This is not difficult to achieve. One important thing to remember is how to signal the beginning of the subordinate clause through the use of the comma, with another comma to signal the end of the clause. If the subordinate clause forms the end of the sentence, it will finish, of course, with a full stop. Where students sometimes go wrong is that they fail to read a sentence back to themselves, to see whether the subordinate clauses have been subsumed into the sentence in an effective way. The trick is to think a little bit more about the overall shape (and sound) of a sentence. We will turn to the signals that help us introduce subordinate clauses in a minute, but for the moment consider the difference between the raw version of a scientific account here, and the version that is rewritten with a focus on moulding the sentences. This is the simple version:

The brain is an organ. It controls most of the body's activities. It is the only organ able to produce 'intelligent' action.

At one level, there is nothing wrong with this. It does, however, suffer from being a little stilted because all the sentences follow the same pattern. We rewrote it thus:

The brain, the organ which controls most of the body's activities, is the only organ able to produce 'intelligent' action.

Through using a subordinate clause structure, the three simple sentences have been compressed into one, although only two words have actually been lost. It is clear that sentences two and three in the first version are on the same theme as sentence one, that they expand on it, and so it is fairly easy to see how the sentences can be put together naturally and form a more interesting statement.

Subordinating conjunctions

We are likely to be more aware of these procedures if we recognise some of the words that signal, or help us introduce, subordinate clauses. A subordinate clause often begins with a subordinating word. Often these are clauses indicating time:

After looking for a while, my dad gave up the search.

When he was a young man, my dad was very fit.

Since coughing a lot last Christmas, my dad has stopped smoking.

The most common subordinating conjunctions are:

after	once	until
although	since	when
as	than	where
because	that	whereas
if	unless	while

You can, therefore, often be aware that you are setting up a subordinate clause when you use one of these signal words. We should point out that some of these words can also be used as **prepositions** (that is, small words such as *in*, *on*, *by*, *to* that show how two parts of a sentence or clause relate to each other, as in *We ran into the house*). Indeed, many words can perform several functions, which is why grammar can be so elusive. The trick is to remember the main structure rather than all the details: subordinate clauses are attached to main clauses and cannot stand on their own as sentences. (It is worth adding that subordinate clauses, like main clauses, normally contain a subject and a main verb, as distinct from phrases which do not.)

There are other subordinating words for setting up subordinate clauses. These are words such as 'who' that relate or link to someone or something said before. They are called **relative pronouns** – the obvious ones are 'that', 'who', and 'which', but 'whoever' is also included here. For example:

We went over to talk to the old man *who* was fishing.

The use of the subordinate clause introduced by 'who' here enables us to avoid saying 'We went over to talk to the old man. He was fishing.' It is a trivial difference in many ways, but it is on the basis of such minor remoulding of sentences that the most complicated things can be said.

The real test of whether you have grasped subordinate clauses is if you can recognise them. Here is a simple sentence: ***Miss Brooke was beautiful***. Here is a complex sentence (the opening sentence of George Eliot's novel *Middlemarch*):

> Miss Brooke had that kind of beauty which seems to be thrown into relief by poor dress.

The logic of this is easy to work out. A sentence starts with a subject. The subject of this sentence is Miss Brooke. It then advances some information about the subject. The simple sentence merely points out that she was beautiful, whereas the complex sentence modifies the statement or adds additional ideas. As in this example, the sentence must rely upon subordinate-clause signal words (in this case ***which***) to expand the idea and include the extra information.

We do not want to set too many exercises in this book since our prime concern is to explain basic points in a clear fashion. You might, however, wish to try this one. Write down ten facts about your life in the form of ten single sentences. For example, sentences such as these:

> I was born in 1977.

> I was born in Harrow.

> I went to school in Harrow.

Then see if you can compress them into fewer sentences but conveying all the same information:

> I was born in 1977, in Harrow, where I also went to school.

As you can see from our example here, the moment you begin doing this you will not only start constructing compound sentences ('I was born and went to school in Harrow') but also complex sentences, involving subordinate clauses. Our feeling is that if you can spot the use of subordinate clauses in texts that you are reading, and spot the use of them in your own work – even though you might not know all the technical terms, or know precisely where the subordinate clauses start and stop – you will be that much more confident about writing complex sentences. The use of subordinate clauses in your sentences will lead towards better writing and, as such, better marks. At the same time, using subordinate clauses or writing compound sentences will cure the bad habits of using comma splices and sentence fragments.

▶ Summary

If you have read this chapter with an eye on how to improve your writing, you should have acquired a reasonable understanding of the following:

▶ The structure of a simple sentence:
  The dog bit the man.
  (subject–verb–object)

▶ The structure of a compound sentence:
  The dog bit the man and then ran off.
  (Two main clauses joined by 'and')

▶ The principle of how to employ subordinate constructions in order to make complex sentences:
  The dog, which had never been known to be vicious, bit the man.
  (Main clause plus subordinate clause)

▶ How to avoid fragments, comma splices, and fused sentences (use conjunctions, absorb the material into the sentence, or begin a new sentence).

These are the basics of writing well; the only other principles are punctuation – in order to signal to the reader how to read your sentences – and the use of the appropriate words (which includes words that are spelt correctly). It is punctuation and spelling that we go on to discuss in the next two chapters.

2 Punctuation

Punctuation is important. It is an essential part of the signalling-system of language and is central to effective communication – as well as to the passing of exams. A lot of people, however, make an awful mess of punctuation, which means that their performance in essays suffers and that they fail to do themselves justice. Yet the basic principles of punctuation are straightforward. The three main punctuation marks it is necessary to grasp are the full stop (we'll include the question mark here), the comma and the apostrophe. These are the equivalent of stopping, changing gear and indicating when driving, and are no more difficult to master than these basic driving skills. There is more to the business of punctuation than just these three points (which is why we return to the subject in chapters 5 and 8), but it is possible to be a clear and successful writer without venturing to use anything as complicated as a semicolon in your written work. The full stop, the comma and the apostrophe, though, are vital, and you must come to terms with how to use them. Correct punctuation will help you say exactly what you want to say in an essay. It will do this because it is concerned with making your meaning clearer by signalling the relationship between words or ideas and also with marking out the boundaries of meaning. There is, too, the further bonus that good punctuation will help create a positive impression of careful and thoughtful work.

▶ Full stops (and question marks)

We will start with the assumption that everyone knows that you start a sentence with a capital letter and end it with a full stop (Americans say 'period'). Students, however, sometimes ignore these most basic guidelines. When we have questioned them about this, they have said that they were concentrating on the content of their work and did not have time to look at the punctuation. The trouble is that this fails to take account of the fact that you are always, except when making notes for yourself, writing for an audience. The person marking your work cannot separate content and form; most markers will allow you a few slips and errors, but if it becomes clear that every sentence has some kind of fault in it, then they will start to lose confidence in your ideas. By contrast, if they can see you have got the measure of writing, then they will respond positively to your work.

But do students really miss out full stops and capital letters? The strict answer is 'no': most students are very sensible and know that they have to obey the basic rules. What does happen, however, is that these rules are broken under pressure in exams and the full stop is replaced as the main punctuation mark by the comma. This is something we dealt with in the previous chapter in the discussion of the comma splice, where the writer adds a comma and then tags another clause or sentence on. Here is a typical example:

> Napoleon's aggression soon led to a resumption of hostilities with Britain, but his preparations for invasion were abandoned after the battle of Trafalgar, Napoleon then marched into Vienna, and beat the Austrians and Russians at Austerlitz (1805), these two blows established his empire.

We have returned to the comma splice (and will come back to it again) because it is such a common failing and so easy to slip into. In the example above, the examination candidate has forgotten that essays need to be written in sentences, and that the units of thought need to be clearly signalled to the reader. A correct version would be:

> Napoleon's aggression soon led to a resumption of hostilities with Britain, but his preparations for invasion were abandoned after the battle of Trafalgar. Napoleon then marched into Vienna, and beat the Austrians and Russians at Austerlitz (1805). These two blows established his empire.

Make sure, therefore, that your work, as in this corrected example, is in sentences, with full stops.

The full stop marks the longest pause in reading. A unit of information has been advanced; the reader then pauses, before passing on to the next unit of information. The only time that you do not use a full stop at the end of a sentence is when you use a question mark. Very rarely, you might wish to conclude a sentence in a formal essay with an exclamation mark, but really the exclamation mark is reserved for use on holiday postcards:

> Just arrived! It's lush! The hotel is great! The food is brilliant! The weather is amazingly hot! Love Sharon and Mark.

Academic work tends to be more understated than other forms of writing, and generally, therefore, exclamation marks are best avoided. The way in which you express yourself in a sentence should give sufficient emphasis if emphasis is called for. Of course, if you are writing for another purpose, such as creating a piece of dramatic narrative, you may well want to have a dialogue full of exclamation marks.

▶ Question marks

The question mark, unlike the exclamation mark, is essential, and something you must take care to include when it is required:

> Did Napoleon represent a real threat to Britain?

Whenever you ask a direct question in your writing, you need to include a question mark: *Can I borrow your bike? Is your name Marco? Does metal expand when heated? Is the Pope Catholic?* It is sometimes a little more difficult to remember that you are asking a question if you construct a complex sentence with subordinate clauses that delay the arrival of the question:

> The question is, given British naval superiority and the fact that Britain is an island, did Napoleon represent a real threat to Britain?

It is all too easy to forget about the question mark at the end of a long sentence like this, and, indeed, it could be argued that its presence or absence does not make a lot of difference. But try to remember to include it, as this is an indication to your reader that you are paying close attention to the form of what you are writing. But be careful. If we had written, 'The question remains as to whether or not Napoleon represented a real threat to Britain', then this is not asking a question as such. The word 'question' in the sentence could be replaced by the word 'problem' or 'issue'. Secondly, we need to distinguish direct questions – *Did Napoleon represent a real threat to Britain?* – from indirect questions: *Students sometimes wonder whether Napoleon posed a real threat to Britain.*

One additional complication is the series of short sentences, or the question mark popping up in the wrong place:

Was Napoleon really so fearsome? and why did he cause such trepidation?

This should be either: *Was Napoleon really so fearsome? Why did he cause such trepidation?* Or: *Was Napoleon really so fearsome, and why did he cause such trepidation?* Except in some very specific circumstances too rare to go into, a question mark cannot suddenly appear in the middle of a sentence. The logic of the question mark, then, is exactly the same as that of the full stop: it comes at the end of the sentence and is followed by a capital letter.

▶ Commas

The full stop indicates a total pause. The comma indicates a lesser pause or slight change of direction in a sentence. Do note, however, that commas cannot be sprinkled over the page at random. Nor do they appear only when a sentence has wandered on for a bit and the writer feels like slipping a comma in to signal a pause. On the contrary, there are precise rules about where commas appear, and, far from being a nuisance, if deployed confidently they can give a lot more impact to what you are saying and greatly increase the complexity, or subtlety, of a sentence. Commas usually separate elements of a sentence. The most obvious example is if you have a sentence that makes a point, but then adds another clause after a subordinating conjunction. For example:

The Jones family moved from Edinburgh to Cardiff. The Macmillan family moved from London to Edinburgh.

We can readily turn these simple sentences into a complex sentence:

The Jones family moved from Edinburgh to Cardiff, whereas the Macmillan family moved from London to Edinburgh.

The comma and the word **whereas** make the transition to the subordinate clause.

At this point, however, some of our readers will say, isn't that just the same as the comma splice that you have warned us about? It is not the same, however; the difference is the use here of the additional word **whereas**, which reshapes and redirects the sentence by serving to introduce the subordinate clause. A useful point of style is to make yourself aware of the existence of these 'enabling' words – other common ones are *although*, *if*, *since*, *unless*, *until* and *while* – that make the transition in sentences, or hold sentences together. Such words will often be combined with commas, to indicate the kind of change of direction, or pull in the opposite direction, that creates an attractive pattern in the shape of a sentence.

The importance of commas should become a little more apparent if you consider these examples of sentences where the writer failed to include commas as required and in the right places, or put them in the wrong places. Not only is a pattern and shape sacrificed in the sentences, but the meaning of the sentences also starts to disintegrate, as the reader is not being steered along tightly enough. Look at how confusing this passage is:

> The period from 1500 to 1640 which can be covered by the use of the term 'Renaissance' is one of changing values, it is a period influenced by progressive ideas that challenged the fixed order of the medieval world so displacing human beings from their position in the cosmos.

We can correct three different kinds of error here:

> The period from 1500 to 1640, which can be covered by the use of the term 'Renaissance', is one of changing values. It is a period influenced by progressive ideas that challenged the fixed order of the medieval world, so displacing human beings from their position in the cosmos.

In the first sentence, we need to insert a pair of commas around *which can be covered by the use of the term 'Renaissance'*: the commas signal that this information is not essential and could be taken away without wrecking the sentence. A second sentence now begins with 'It' whereas before what we had was a comma splice. Finally, we have inserted a comma before *so*, marking the introduction of the subordinate clause, but not before *that challenged the fixed order of the medieval world*, also a subordinate clause, because these words provide essential information identifying what is being talked about and cannot be taken away without destroying the sense of the sentence.

This might seem very fussy and complicated. All we have said so far, however, is that you must include commas when required in order to steer your reader through a sentence in the right way. 'But where are commas required?' you might ask. 'How do I know when to include them?' In order to make it as clear as possible, we have reduced this in the next section to the six rules that govern the comma.

▶ The six uses of the comma

1. Punctuating linked main clauses

A string of simple sentences can quickly become boring:

> Nigel is a real man. He smokes cigarettes. He drinks lager. He reads men's magazines. He has one GCSE.

The easiest way of making this slightly more interesting for the reader is to introduce compound sentences. For example:

> Nigel is a real man. He smokes cigarettes and drinks lager.

There is no need for a comma in the second sentence here, however, as there is such a simple structure using the conjunction *and* to join the original two parallel short sentences. Note, however, the change of meaning a comma can produce: *I like fish and chips* means I like fish and chips together; *I like fish, and chips* means I like fish, and I also like chips. If the second clause moves on to a fresh idea, a comma might well be necessary to indicate a division between the two main clauses:

> I like fish and chips, and every Friday night I buy some for my tea.

The cases where two main clauses are linked almost always involve the use of *and*, *but* or *or*.

One complication is that in short sentences the comma is not always necessary. Consider this: we might have two sentences: *The sun tans. The sun burns*. It is much more effective if you write *The sun tans but it also burns*. In this case the comma seems superfluous. Indeed, some people argue that you do not need a comma before a co-ordinating conjunction. It is, however, perfectly acceptable to write *The sun tans, but it also burns*. If in doubt about whether to include the comma when linking two main clauses with *and* or *but*, the best advice is to include it. In our earlier example, you would not be making a mistake if you wrote:

> Nigel is a real man. He smokes cigarettes, and drinks lager.

It is just a little over-fussy when the sentence is short, and when the units of the sentence do not need separating all that much as there is no real danger of confusing your reader. Punctuation, remember, is all about clarity, about making sure your reader understands what you have written.

To finish this section, we will end with a sentence that illustrates how a comma is used as the punctuation mark in a sentence where two main clauses are being linked. *That is the first use of the comma, and it is a straightforward one*.

2. Setting off the introductory element of a sentence

Another instance in which the comma is necessary is to set off the intro-ductory elements of a sentence. We can illustrate this by considering that last sentence. The subject of the sentence is *Another instance in which the comma is necessary*. We could have started the paragraph, however, with an introductory clause:

> If we move on to the second use of the comma, we can consider another instance in which the comma is necessary to set off the introductory element of a sentence.

In this example, the introductory element is just a way of establishing a link to ease the reader into the main points being made. The same thinking is in evidence when we use tiny verbal tags such as *Of course* or *Well*:

> Of course, she came first in every race.
> Well, if you have confidence in Smith we can offer her the job.

More commonly, however, we use **prepositional words or phrases** to set up the main sentence. Prepositions are words, mostly short ones, that show how other words relate to each other. A prepositional phrase, therefore, is a phrase at the start of a sentence that eases the reader from one sentence to the next or eases the reader into a sentence. 'Preposition' literally means 'to go before', establishing a position, as in these examples:

> *Around* the world, five out of ten people consume alcohol.

> *Up* on the roof, the tiles were showing signs of wear.

> *Near* the seaside, the temperature is often lower.

> *After* selling her business, she was a millionairess.

Why, you might ask, do we use a comma after these introductory phrases? The point is that it helps clarify the meaning of a sentence, the very slight pause in reading allowing the reader to shift from finding a position to focusing on the real substance of the sentence without confusion. The comma divides the information up so that the reader can absorb it in meaningful units. The rule to bear in mind, then, is a fairly simple one. At the beginning of a sentence, you might encounter an introductory or prepositional phrase that is set off by a comma.

3. Additional and subordinate clauses at the end of sentences

We often add another clause at the end of a sentence, most commonly a subordinate clause. It adds to the meaning of the main clause, but cannot stand on its own. Here is a simple sentence:

Television programmes for teenagers are usually embarrassing.

We might want to extend the sentence:

Television programmes for teenagers are usually embarrassing, although some are excellent.

The comma is used before the subordinate clause in order to clarify the meaning by making the sentence easier and clearer to read. The difficulty is that a comma is not always absolutely necessary. To some extent it depends upon you deciding whether a slight pause or change of direction needs to be signalled to the reader. If in doubt, include the comma. You should, however, always make sure that it is separating elements of a sentence; that is to say, most often it will appear at the start and/or end of a clause, and not between the subject and verb unless an adverb has been inserted. In the example we have provided here, the person who got it wrong would probably write:

Television programmes for teenagers, are usually embarrassing although some are excellent.

There are two mistakes here, though they just involve the one comma. The first is the failure to insert the comma between clauses – that is after *embarrassing* – which is where it should come. Very often students sense a comma is needed but then – and this is the second mistake – they put it, as here, between the subject (*Television programmes for teenagers*) and the verb (*are*). This is always wrong: *The dog, bit the man* is incorrect. It should be: *The dog bit the man*. As we noted above, the only time you separate the subject from the verb is when you insert an adverb or a phrase: *The man, oddly enough, bit the dog in return*.

4. Subordinating and parenthetical elements inserted in a sentence

Parenthetical expressions in a sentence are those little words like *however* and *therefore* which we slip in to make one sentence flow into or link up with the next. There is a whole range of these, including *of course, for example, indeed, in fact*, and *nevertheless*. They are almost always set off by bracketing or isolating commas used in pairs: *The game was won, however, in the last minute*. Of course, if the words or phrase come at the start of the sentence, there is only a single comma: *In fact, the painting was lost for many years*.

There is, however, one mistake many students make. An extra word or clause inserted in the body of a sentence must be set up and conclude with a comma. The opening sentence of this paragraph cannot be written as:

> There is however, one mistake many students make.

Note, therefore, the comma both before and after *however*. It is essential to have a comma both sides of the parenthetical expression. In a similar way, a subordinate clause introduced in a sentence must start and end with a comma:

> This section on commas, which by now is probably becoming a bit of a bore, has only two more rules to explain.

This sentence, which is the last sentence of this paragraph, illustrates the punctuation convention for a subordinate clause within the body of a sentence.

5. Appositives

Most people have never heard the word 'appositive', but it is very easy to get into a muddle in handling them without knowing it. An appositive is a noun or phrase that renames another noun just before it:

> Sarah King, Britain's oldest woman, will be 112 next week.

Britain's oldest woman renames Sarah King, so is set off by commas. Where students get in a muddle is with book titles or other titles.

> Hardy's final novel, *Jude the Obscure*, is dark and gloomy.
> Brontë's first work, *Jane Eyre*, was swiftly followed by *Villette*.

Be careful to use the commas only when renaming. In this example, you don't need one before *Villette*, but you would if you had written:

> Brontë's first novel, *Jane Eyre*, was swiftly followed by her best novel, *Villette*.

6. Commas between items in a series, and between two or more adjectives that equally modify the same word

Lots of people more or less know about this convention, but are often unsure about one of the finer points. In relation to items in a series, we would usually write

For breakfast I always have bacon, egg and fried bread.

April, June, September and November all have 30 days.

In both cases, we have inserted commas between the elements of a series, but omitted the comma before the co-ordinating conjunction *and* (*egg and fried bread*). This is standard practice, particularly in Britain. Americans, however, tend to insert the comma before the *and*, and it is perfectly legitimate, indeed helpful, to do so if it helps clarify the overall meaning. For example:

She sold all kinds of rare, unusual, and cheap and cheerful gifts.

We use a comma between adjectives when they modify the same word equally:

I looked at his old, haggard face.

The comma in this instance could, in fact, be replaced by *and*. We do not use a comma, however, when the adjective next to the noun is more closely related to the noun in meaning:

Catherine has several part-time jobs.

If you are unsure, the obvious answer is to put a comma where *and* would sound right. There are other rules governing the use of commas, but we do not want to overwhelm you with too much information. The main thing to remember is that you are not using commas for the sake of using commas, but to highlight and direct the meaning of what you are saying. There are rules, but common sense is also involved: you have to judge where the pauses and changes of pace come in a sentence, and make the appropriate gesture. The key is to think about why and where and how commas are used, following the broad guidelines outlined above.

▶ The apostrophe

We came across a newsagent's once called 'Apostrophe S'. We had a vision of the sign-writer not knowing whether to write *Harry's* or *Harrys'* or *Harrys* or *Harries* and in the end deciding there was less chance of making a mistake if he called it 'Apostrophe S'. The apostrophe does certainly seem to cause an immense amount of grief. If you want to see how not to use the apostrophe, visit your local greengrocer, where almost inevitably *Tomatoe's* and *Potatoe's* will be on sale instead of *Tomatoes* and *Potatoes*. Perhaps you receive the *Lands' End* catalogue; they at least know that they are using it incorrectly, that it should be *Land's End*, but they have decided to continue with their founder's initial mistake. So why is there all this difficulty and fuss with the apostrophe? If it causes so much trouble, why bother? Well, correct use of the apostrophe does clarify meaning, but perhaps just as important is that correct use of the apostrophe signals to your reader that you have a clear command of the conventions of writing. In the end, the apostrophe is like good manners and a smart appearance; they might not be all that important in themselves, but they could be the things that made the crucial difference if you were applying for a job.

The first thing to grasp about apostrophes is that they differ from other punctuation marks. Other punctuation marks are used to separate words or clauses. The apostrophe, however, appears as part of a word. It indicates either possession or the omission of one or more letters. That is, it has two different functions and two different meanings which we will explain below. We also try our very best to explain how the two meanings get confused. It is something of a long story.

The possessive and singular nouns

We can start with the very basic and simple use of the apostrophe, and that is to indicate something belongs to someone. This is what we mean by the possessive. So, for example, we can say *This is Jane's book*. It should be plain that this means the book belongs to Jane: the form *Jane's*, using the apostrophe before the *s*, indicates ownership or belonging to. So, to construct the possessive with a singular noun we add *'s*.

We deal with other examples of the possessive below, but the key lesson to learn here has to do with singular nouns. It is almost insulting to explain this, but if no one ever tells you that the word *dog* is singular whereas the word *dogs* is plural, how are you supposed to know? Singular means just one, while plural means more than one. The *s* in the *'s*, however, has nothing to do with making anything plural. This is a crucial point to grasp. There are two distinct operations to keep separate: one is how to make nouns plural, the other how to indicate the possessive. They get confused because they both involve the letter *s*.

Let's take another example. This is an extract from an essay by a student at university studying English:

Austens *Persuasion* tells the story of Annes love for Captain Wentworth, Lady Russells opposition to their marriage, and Annes quiet victory.

Here a whole set of apostrophes is missing. It should read:

Austen's *Persuasion* tells the story of Anne's love for Captain Wentworth, Lady Russell's opposition to their marriage, and Anne's quiet victory.

The apostrophe needs to be inserted after the singular names here to indicate possession. Possession in relation to the apostrophe is a broad term. We might see that **Anne's book** is obviously a possessive – that is, the book belongs to Anne, it is hers, she owns it – but **Anne's love** is also possessive – it means the love of Anne, her love. If in doubt, it is always possible to turn the phrase round, and write it another way:

The story of the love of Anne for Captain Wentworth

But the basic rule is that **'s** means something belonging to the word before the apostrophe. **Chelsea's away-strip is new again this season** means that the away-strip of Chelsea is new again this season. The basic rule, then, is that we have a singular noun – **Anne** or **Chelsea** – and all we do is add **'s** to that noun when we want to talk about something that belongs to her or it, or is part of her or it.

The possessive and plural nouns and proper names
The difficulty over the apostrophe starts when we move on to plural nouns. The problem arises from thinking that the apostrophe has something to do with making words plural. It does not. To repeat the point we made earlier: adding **'s** has nothing to do with making words plural.

We usually make nouns plural by adding **s**; so, for example, *cat* becomes *cats*; *student* becomes *students*. There are, though, some words which make their plurals differently: the plural of *child* is *children*; *leaf* becomes *leaves*; *kiss* becomes *kisses*; *mouse* becomes *mice*. Most nouns, however, form plurals simply by adding **s** to the singular.

Where students usually get in a muddle – if this applies to you, read slowly at this point – is with the apostrophe when there is a plural noun. There is, though, no need for confusion. The basic rule is that you add **'s** to form a possessive. Thus:

The children's party had to be cancelled.

This means that the party of the children had to be cancelled: the plural noun is *children*. With this example we can compare the following, all adding *'s*: *George's essay*, *France's territory*, *somebody's dog*, *men's ties*, *women's rights*.

Three exceptions

There are just three places where this basic rule does not apply. First, if the plural noun already ends in *s*, we only add an apostrophe:

> The teachers' strike showed no sign of ending.

> The pupils' education was being disrupted.

> It was several years' work down the drain.

In each of these cases the word before the apostrophe is plural: *teachers*, *pupils*, *years*. If we take the first example, we can see that it is about the strike of more than one teacher – it is the strike of several teachers. A way of decoding this is to say that we know it is plural because we have added only an apostrophe: the *s* comes before the apostrophe, so the base word is *teachers*. If it were just one teacher, we would write *the teacher's strike*: here the *s* comes after the apostrophe, so the base word is *teacher* and we have added *'s*.

The second exception where we add only an apostrophe is with names ending in *s* where we don't pronounce them with an extra *s*. Thus we have:

> Thomas's arrival

but

> Ulysses' journey

What, though, if we were talking about the arrival of the whole Thomas family rather than one individual called Thomas? In other words, what if we wanted to discuss the arrival of the Thomases? The plural of *Thomas* is *Thomases*, that is, the plural ends in *s*. Because it does so, we treat it just like the word *teachers*, as a plural noun ending in *s*:

> The Thomases' arrival.

We have included this example because it reinforces how to apply the rule in the case of a plural noun ending in *s* – just add an apostrophe.

The final exception is where we add nothing. We began this section with the confusion in the nation's greengrocers about how to spell the plural word *Potatoes*. We do not add an apostrophe to words to make them plural, but there is also another set of word where we do not add an apostrophe. These are pronouns:

It is his car. Where are our coats? Whose is this dog? That is hers, but where is my hat? I think this is yours.

Most people know most of these: occasionally a student will writer *her's*, and some students confuse *whose* with the contracted form *who's*, meaning *who is* or *who has*. We deal with contractions below, but there is one more word to add to this list of exceptions which causes more confusion than almost any other word in the English language – the word *its*:

A dog wags its tail.

Here the word *its* acts as a possessive in the same way that the words *my*, *hers* and *ours* do above. There is another word *it's*, but this is not a possessive; instead, *it's* means *it is*. We discuss this further below, but at this point the key thing to remember is that the word *its* means 'belonging to it'. There is no such word as *its'*. If you write *its'*, however accidental the slip, those reading your work will immediately notice it and wonder why you have not avoided one of the commonest errors in writing. The answer is to tell yourself we **never** write *its'*, that we never place an apostrophe at the end of the word *its*.

Omission of letters or contraction

As we noted above, we also use the apostrophe mark to indicate the omission in a standard contraction. We'd better explain the rule about this in some detail as this is where a good deal of the chaos over punctuation starts. If we had to identify one area that creates problems for students, it would be this idea of contractions – that is, where a word is shortened and an apostrophe is used to indicate this.

It's

The first point to repeat is that the apostrophe has two different functions. One, as we have seen above at great length, is for the possessive case: *It is Jane's book*. But then the apostrophe is also used in a different way with a different meaning when we use it to indicate a contraction. The most famous contraction, and the one that sinks a thousand exam scripts, is when, instead of writing *it is*, we write *it's*. Here the apostrophe signals that the two words *it* and *is* have been contracted into one word and that a letter has been omitted: *it's*, then, means *it is*, or, in some cases, *it has*: *It's been raining here all day*.

Its

Many students know this, but then, often without thinking, they remember that somewhere they have seen a word *its* which is a personal possessive pronoun: *the dog wags its tail*. If you are guilty of this – in other words, if you are the sort of person who writes *the dog wags it's tail* – there is only way out of the muddle. This is to learn that *it's* **always means** *it is* or *it has*. Some teachers would go further than this and suggest that the only safe way to avoid making the error is never to write *it's*. In other words, they suggest that, in order to stop yourself getting in a mess, you should always write *it is* and never contract them into a single word. If you learn that, then you should be able to learn that there is only one form of *its*, and that is *its*.

The difficulty with this advice, though sound, is that *it is* can sound very formal, and it may not be possible to follow it all the time. Again, few people say *it is*, and the force of speech and common usage to change language is considerable. Indeed, it seems not at all unlikely that in time the distinctions between it's and its will disappear. In the meantime, however, it is as well to learn the difference.

Quite a lot of people disapprove of the use of contractions in essay writing, or in a book. We have used them because they give an informal air, but some stylists would frown at all of the following contractions:

he's for *he is*

she's for *she is*

let's for *let us*

doesn't for *does not*

won't for *will not*

weren't for *were not*

it's for *it is*

who's for *who is*

The advice to avoid these contractions is good advice and well meant. But we all live in the real world where these contractions are used millions of times a day both in speech and writing. The uncontracted forms are inevitably becoming more and more rare, perhaps because they sound stilted. The advice, then, has to be do not use these forms if you are someone who gets them wrong. If you do get them wrong, don't give up trying to sort them out. After all, it is not really your fault if a phrase such as *Harry's home* can mean both *Harry is home* and *The home belonging to Harry*. The context will tell you what is meant: in the first instance, where it means *Harry is home*, the verb *is* has been contracted; in the second instance, *Harry's* is the possessive form. In examples like this, the possessive case and the contraction are identical. But a phrase such as *Jane's book* can only mean the book belonging to Jane: it would make no sense if we tried to make it mean *Jane is book*. There does come a point, in other words, where you have to use your common sense.

▶ Summary

Let's run over again the rules about the apostrophe. The basic rule is add 'apostrophe s' for a simple singular possessive case:

The director's salary rose again this year.

But also for singular words ending in s

Oasis's fame was short-lived.

Los Angeles's weather is great.

But just add the apostrophe when it is a plural noun ending in *s* already:

The stars' party was crowded with no-hopers.

But remember that the apostrophe only appears if it is a possessive. So there is no need for it in

The stars and stripes are a symbol of America.

In this case both stars and stripes are plural nouns but not in the possessive case. The contrast is with *America's stars and stripes are well known*.

The rule about apostrophes and possession is, however, different in relation to personal pronouns. The following words are possessives and have no apostrophe: *hers*, *mine*, *his*, *yours*, *its*, *theirs* and *ours*. These words do not have apostrophes because they are the possessive forms of the words *she*, *I*, *he*, *you*, *it*, *they* and *we*. Let's repeat a key part of this information: it is always *theirs*, never *their's*; it is always *hers*, and never *hers'* or *her's*; always *his* and never *his'*; always *its* and never *its'*. We are going to return to the rule about *its* and *it's* in the next chapter, which is essentially about spelling, because so many people make the *its'/it's* mistake that we feel it is worth repeating ourselves.

For the moment, however, let's take stock. We now have ideas about:

▶ The full stop
▶ The question mark
▶ The six main usages of the comma
▶ The apostrophe

There are other levels of complication to punctuation, but first things first: you are not going to get the other things right if you cannot get these right. Look at the last essay you wrote; read it from a point of view of punctuation. Are you sure that stops and commas are as they should be? Is your use of apostrophes confident or simply embarrassing? An hour spent looking at your own work – essentially, marking yourself – will do a lot to sharpen your grasp of the rules.

3 Spelling

Points covered
- ▶ **Sound-alike words**
- ▶ **Avoidable errors**
- ▶ **How words end**
- ▶ **Summary**

Writing is a craft, and as with any craft it has to be learned. Or should that be 'learnt'? Which is the correct word? Writing is all about using the correct words in the correct order. So far, we have concentrated on the mechanics of achieving the right word order in a sentence. Now, however, we want to turn to getting the words themselves right.

There are several aspects to this. One is finding the right tone. There is, in itself, nothing wrong with phrases such as *well hard*, but it would probably strike a rather jarring note in a formal essay if you wrote that *Julius Caesar was well hard, a diamond geezer*. Using the appropriate word – and finding the right level – is an issue we return to in chapter 9. The more fundamental difficulty, however, is that of knowing, or not knowing, how to spell words. In some ways this is becoming less of a problem in students' work because they can confirm their spelling on a computer's spell-check. This is obviously a useful tool and can be used interactively to improve spelling in addition to correcting inaccurate word-processing. There is, however, also a negative side to relying on a computer, especially for spelling quite common words since it is these that are often misspelt in exams. We deal in chapter 6, therefore, with a host of words that students will find it helpful to know how to spell. There is, though, another category of words that a spell-check will not be able to identify as errors. *Their* and *there* are both English words, but a spell-check will not be able to tell you which word you need to use in a particular context. Confusion between *their* and *there* is, in fact, one of the most common slips in all writing. We have, therefore, put it at the head of the 'Top Twenty Spelling Errors' list that forms the basis of this chapter. Every one of these mistakes is made thousands of times every day, in everything from essays to advertising brochures, from letters to circulars. Because they are common mistakes they stand out all the more in formal writing. So, if you have difficulty with spelling – and one of the authors of this book is not too embarrassed to admit that he has to work at his spelling – try to come to terms with this Top Twenty. It is divided into three sections, starting with words that sound the same. Obviously, if you know how to spell all of the words that follow, you will probably skim this chapter, but you might glance at each topic to make sure. Correct spelling is an area that is easy to overlook, and under-estimate, in terms of its effect on the reader or marker of your writing.

▶ Sound-alike words

1. *Their and there*
Just because two words sound the same does not mean they have the same meaning or, indeed, that there is any kind of connection between them at all. The main thing to remember about *there* is that it is not *here*. In other words, *there* is a location. *Their*, on the other hand, means belonging to them (*it is their house*), and as such is a possessive.

It is quite easy to remember that three words indicating a place or pointing out something all have *here* in them:

> here, there, where

As a quick rule of thumb, when you are about to choose *there* or *their*, ask yourself whether it is a place or person that is being referred to:

> There is a weakness in their game; their passing is awful, and there seems no way to improve it or their co-ordination.

> 'There, there,' said their father, 'there's no need to cry', as he tried to console the children for the loss of their rabbit. 'It may be over there, in the fields.'

Another related word that you might be tempted to use is *they're*, which is a contraction of *they are* and is pronounced the same as *there* and *their*. As we noted in the previous chapter, contractions lend an air of informality to writing, but in an academic essay it is more appropriate to use the full form *they are* rather than *they're*.

2. Effect/affect; accept/except
The words *effect* and *affect* are widely used (and confused) in students'

essays, largely because they are often describing how changes take place, in novels, in a test-tube or in life, that bring about a certain effect or a certain result:

> The effect of mixing the two chemicals was a huge explosion that killed half the class.

Effect here means the consequence, the result of something. It can also be used as a verb, meaning to bring about:

> He effected a change in government policy.

Affect, however, means to have an influence on somebody or something, usually on feelings:

> The remaining members of the class were much affected by the tragedy.

Affect, then, is a verb meaning 'to influence', 'to be moved by', whereas *effect*, meaning results, is usually a noun. The most reliable check is to see whether there is *a*, *an* or *the* in front of the word; if there is, it is not a verb, and so the correct word will probably be *effect*:

> They were all deeply affected by the effect of the explosion.

If you are not certain, therefore, whether you have used the right word, look at the word before: was it *a*, *an* or *the*? An error in the same area is confusion between *accept* and *except*. Again, *accept* is a verb, meaning 'to receive willingly', whereas *except* means 'excluding' or 'but':

> All accepted the free samples of chocolates, except those on a diet.

3. Principal/principle

This is another pair of words that are often confused, and where it is worth making the effort to distinguish between them on the basis of what you know. In science, for example, you may be writing about the principal effects of something (meaning the foremost effects), while, in history or philosophy, you may be concerned with moral principles. *Principal* means 'main' (Americans use *principal* as a term for the head of a school); *principle* is a rule, value or standard. We could, therefore, write that *The principal is a man with certain principles*.

A way of remembering these kinds of difference is through the use of mnemonics, a made-up phrase to aid memory. The mnemonic might be more trouble than it is worth, but the combination of letters in the following, for example, might remind you of the difference between *principal* and *principle*:

My number one pal is the principal.

Disciples have principles.

Principal, however, is not just a person:

His principal reason for leaving the country was to visit his mother.

In each case, *principal* means or is connected with the main or foremost quality of something.

4. Practice/practise

These two are constantly muddled up. That might seem an exaggerated claim, but even as we revised this book we came across this in *The Times Higher Education Supplement*: 'The institute has got to justify itself and we are now agreed we are not looking to issue a licence to practice.' The licence being discussed is a licence to teach; what the article should have said is 'a licence to practise'. *Practice* is a noun, *practise* is a verb. Doctors, therefore, work at their practice where they practise their trade. In the same way, you practise your violin, but you do it during something that is your violin practice. If there is an active element of doing something, it is the verb, *practise*; if, however, it is just a description of the activity, rather than actually doing the activity, it is *practice*. You should therefore:

Practise the piano, because practice makes perfect.

Another way of checking is to remember the two words *device* and *devise*, where there is the same distinction between noun and verb, but the sound is different enough to prevent them being confused. In America, we might note, the practice is different: they only use *practice*. Words such as *advice* and *advise* also have the same pattern of difference between the noun and the verb as do *practice* and *practise*. Really, all you have to remember is that there are two forms, a noun (*-ice*) and a verb (*-ise*). The confusion largely arises because people do not know that there are both.

▶ Stop and check

We might have spent a lot of time over a few words, but these are extremely common mistakes. Our feeling is that if you stop and check these words, then you are likely also to be much more careful in general about spelling. In many cases it is a question of noticing, and then checking and finding out. The best spellers take nothing for granted: they use their dictionaries; they make up mnemonics to help them. Perhaps above all, they try to make sure they understand why words are spelt the way they are, whether they are the noun form or a possessive, for instance. Before moving on, we want to offer a very contrived sentence that includes all the examples so far. Can you see why each option is as it is?

Their principal effect on the practice of the new doctors was to affect the principles practised there.

5. Miscellaneous sound-alikes

What follows is a short list of words that are quite often misused in essays, and which give a poor impression of the writer's competence. They are, then, things to watch out for and avoid. When, for example, a student writes: *I didn't here the telephone ring*, the effect is to puzzle the reader for a moment. It should, of course, be *hear* (if you cannot remember, think of your *ear*), whereas *here* is a place, as in *here*, *there* and *everywhere*.

There are other pairs of words, too, that can easily get confused. We *know* things, because one has knowledge, whereas *no* is the opposite of yes. A car has a *brake*, to slow it down or stop it, but actors are said to *break* a leg. That you *lead* a horse to water, but if you did it yesterday, you would have *led* the horse to water; the difference here is between present and past tense. There's past and present again in the next pairing: choose/chose. *Choose* is present tense, whereas you *chose* to do something yesterday. They sound very similar, but *loose* and *lose* differ from *choose* and *chose* and really need to be learnt: people wear loose clothes, but they lose football matches (if stuck, there's room for two o's in loose; it's a loose-fitting kind of word in itself). *Quiet* and *quite*, on the other hand, should not be confused, as they actually sound different: *Before I went on my quiet diet, I could take quite a bite out of any cake.* And children should be *seen* and not heard, whereas *scene* is a part of a play or a pleasant view.

In all these cases, you have to learn to use your resources of language and common sense to get the right word for the right job. The confusion of *led* (part tense of the verb to lead) and the metal *lead* (pronounced *led*) is a good test of whether you understand that some words share sounds, some share spelling, but can differ in function and meaning.

6. To/too/two; were/where; are/our

To/too/two
The difference between to and *too* is perhaps easy to remember. First of all, bear in mind that *two* is a number. That leaves only *too* and *to* to sort out. In contexts where you want to say 'more than enough' or 'also' the word to use is *too*:

> I am too embarrassed to admit it.

> The teacher was too strict.

In these examples, *too* means 'more than enough'. The 'also' meaning will often appear when *too* is at the end of a sentence: *The rest of my family decided to come too*.
   In all other structures you use *to*:

> To know her is to admire her.

> I would like to be his double.

In both these examples *to* is used with the base form of the verb ('admire', 'be') to form the infinitive. This is probably its commonest usage.

Were/where
This pair is again worth getting right. *Where* is a place (one of these three: *here*, *there*, *where*); *were* is a verb:

> We were on our way home to where we feel we belong.

You might say this sentence so as to stress the *h* in *where*. Sometimes mistakes with similar-sounding words or words that look alike can be overcome by using pronunciation to help fix an aspect in your head. In general, though, pronunciation is not a very reliable guide to spelling.

Are/our
Are is a verb, whereas *our* indicates possession:

> We are here to collect our possessions.

These little mistakes – confusing *are* and *our* together with *were* and *where* – are errors that it is easy to slip into but which can be avoided if you are alert to them. They do damage the impression your work makes on the reader, particularly if they occur throughout an essay. Check every time that you use them until getting them right becomes automatic.

7. Compliment/complement

Finally in this first section: *compliment* and *complement*. These are words that businesses seem inexplicably drawn to use in letters, but which they more often than not get wrong. *Complement* completes something or brings it to perfection or matches it. A *compliment* is words of praise. As we say, many business letters confuse these distinctions, and the result is usually very funny. If someone writes

The shirt complimented his tie

they are trying to say they go well together. But what they are actually saying is that the shirt said to the tie 'You're rather silky.' It should be *The shirt complemented his tie*, with an *e*. If you are feeling particularly full of yourself the next time you are in a restaurant, you might want to send your compliments to the chef; that is, you are praising someone for their cooking. If, on the other hand, you 'complemented' the chef, it would mean that you made a good team together – the chef cooking, you washing up.

▶ Avoidable errors

8. It's/its

We dealt with the distinction between *it's* and *its* in the last chapter, but want to return to it here, as a spelling problem, because it is so common an error in students' writing. The most important thing to remember is that there is no such form as *its'*. *Its* is one of a few words that are already possessives, and do not, therefore, need an apostrophe adding to them: These possessive words are

my/mine	its
your/yours	our/ours
his	their/theirs
her/hers	whose

As we noted in the last chapter, *it's* is two words ('it is' or 'it has') contracted into one: it has nothing to do with the possessive. *It's* is used in a large number of situations, but it is by far the best policy to avoid contractions (words such as *can't*, *don't* and *won't*) in formal essays, as these are colloquial forms of the words and therefore not entirely appropriate. Some writers, it has to be said, disagree. There is, though, a further danger with contractions: if you forget to put the apostrophe in, for example, 'can't', you end up writing 'cant'.

We hope by now, therefore, that you can you see the sense of avoiding writing *it's* and instead using *it is* whenever possible:

> It is my dog and it has hurt its leg.

9. Disconnect, dissatisfaction and other 'dis', 'mis' and 'un' words

In tackling spelling questions, there are some things that you may have to learn by rote, but there are others that you can work out for yourself. Sometimes it is a case of sounding out a word to yourself to remind yourself of how it is spelt. At other times, you may be able to work out how a word is formed. This particularly applies to words with *dis* at the beginning. If you add 'dis' at the beginning of a word, it reverses the meaning, so *like* becomes *dislike*. If you *connect* something, you can also *disconnect* something. There is no great spelling problem here until we come on to words such as 'dissatisfaction'. You have added *dis* to *satisfaction*, so there are two *s*'s in the word. In the same way *informed* becomes *misinformed*, but if you *misspell* a word it has two *s*'s in it, because you have added *mis* to *spell*. And *unaware* only has one *n*, because you have added *un* to aware, but in *unnecessary* and *unnoticed* the *un* is an addition to words that start with *n*. So, there are no strange tricks or bits of magic here: you add *dis*, *mis* or *un* to the existing word.

10. Separate, February

Why is it that some words are misspelt by so many? These two are words that people get wrong over and over again. It is *sep-ar-ate*, not *sep-er-ate*. It is *Feb-ru-ary*, not *Feb-u-ary*. The only advice we have is learn them, but particularly *separate*, perhaps by remembering the two *e*'s are separated by two *a*'s.

11. i before e when the sound is ee, except after c

English spelling is hard to become an expert at because it seems so unsystematic. There are, however, some rules that do apply, although the moment one spells out a rule someone will pop up and draw attention to all the words that do not conform to the rule. But '*i* before *e*, except after *c*' is a useful one, because it relates to such a common misspelling in essays: the word *receive*. This is a case where '*i* before *e* except after *c* when the sound is *ee*' applies. It is, of course, also a very catchy rule to commit to memory. We would, therefore, spell words where there is no *c* before-hand in the following manner:

Piece, grief, achieve, siege, shield, priest, mischief.

But, as against these we would have:

conceit, conceive, deceive, deceiver, deceit, receipt, receive, receiver.

But because there is no *ee* sound, you would have words like:

deign, rein, rein, weight, eight.

If we say these sound *weird*, it is only to draw attention to the fact that all words do not conform to the rule, but enough do to make it worth remembering: '*i* before *c* except after *c* when the sound is *ee*'.

12. Double consonants or single consonants?

We are continuing here with problems in the body of a word. How, for example, does one spell a word like **embarrass**? How does one know, if at all, that there are two *r*'s in it? The fact is that there is no simple way of inferring what is correct. There comes a point at which you have to know these things or run a spell-check (or risk getting it wrong). Time and time again, there is no clear way of knowing whether we require a double or a single letter for a consonantal sound. That is why, in chapter 6, we are going to provide a list of the words that are spelt wrongly not just in students' essays but in a whole range of formal documents: words like **accommodate** and **appal**, **committee** and **exaggerate**, **skilful** and **unparalleled**.

But there is one rule for the endings of words, even if it is not instantly memorable. You double the final consonant if you are adding **ing** or **ed** when the word ends in a single consonant which is preceded by a single vowel **and** the accent is on the last syllable. Consequently, we have **begin** and **beginning**, **stop** and **stopping**, but in **unparalleled** above, the emphasis wasn't on the last syllable in the word unparallel. What about adding to **sleep**? It's **sleeping**, because the consonant **p** wasn't preceded by a single vowel. We are aware that the rule here is probably more difficult to grasp than remembering the spelling of words – and in a sense that is where we are directing you. The rules, such as they are, are so extensive that it is a much easier answer to start thinking about your spelling; look harder at how words are spelt, and how you spell words. We'll turn to how some other words end in a moment, but first, while we are on the 'body' of words, we should add something about the use of capital letters and hyphens.

13. Capital letters

This might not seem to be a spelling issue, but in a certain way it is – and getting it wrong can be irritating for the reader. Capital letters exist for proper names: Marie, Oliver, Roberts, Hughes, London, Paris, London Palladium, Royal Opera House, Sydney Harbour Bridge, The Dog and Duck, Lucranos. For some reason, people use capitals far too often. You don't need them for centuries: it is *In the twentieth century*, not *In the Twentieth Century*. The best rule is simply to ask yourself, if in doubt, why you are using the capital letter. The trend is to use them less and less. Today, therefore, most people would write:

> The British prime minister, Tony Blair, had lunch with the chancellor, Gordon Brown.

The main reason given for the use of fewer capital letters is that too many in a piece of writing interrupt the passage of the eye along a line. You would write *government*, *the cabinet*, but *Department of Education* (though this can be avoided by turning it around and making it *the education department*). So, *the English school* at the university would be correct, as would *Brighton's football club*. You would write *the north of England* and *the south of France*, but *East Timor*. If in doubt, underplay rather than overplay capitals.

It might be objected that in this section our advice has veered away from the 'rules' and 'correctness' towards usage and the changing language. The inconsistency, however, is only apparent: there are 'rules' but they are changing at different rates. What seems to make the changes acceptable is the extent to which they are taken up by educated users of English. In that sense the 'rules' remain in place, but modified.

14. Hyphens

We return to hyphens in chapter 6, but here we just want to highlight the adjective convention. You can write *In the nineteenth century, a lot of things changed* with no hyphen, because it is an adjective (nineteenth) and noun (century) phrase. But if you write *In nineteenth-century Britain, a lot of things changed*, you need to use a hyphen because *nineteenth-century* form a compound adjective modifying *Britain* (though it is fair to say that this practice is changing). Generally the rule is that you use a hyphen if it avoids confusion. Hence you would write twelve-inch nails, to make it clear that the nails measured twelve inches rather than you had twelve of them all measuring an inch. As we say, we return to hyphens in chapter 6.

15. Titles, characters' names, proper names, texts, etc.

Teaching a course that included *Vanity Fair* by Thackeray and *Jane Eyre* by Charlotte Brontë, we came across a candidate who wrote about *Vanity Fare* by Thackray and *Jayne Eyre* by Charlote Bronte. This set us thinking about the problem of students who spell the names of books and characters incorrectly, or who spell words that are in the question incorrectly, or if they are examining some medical concept such as *diarrhoea*, spell the name of the disease incorrectly. The advice we have is as follows: English spelling is tricky, but part of studying a topic involves paying careful attention to the actual words that are at the heart of your course. Knowing how to spell the words that are at the core of your subject is also a central part of revision. Some spelling mistakes can be forgiven, but if you are writing about politics and think that *prime minster* is the correct spelling, or if you are studying literature and think there are authors called Charles Dicken's and John Keat's, as against *Charles Dickens* and *John Keats*, your study methods are letting you down. One simple answer is to be wary and take nothing on trust. That, however, comes back to the gist of much of what we have said, which is that spelling is probably in the end about paying attention, noticing things and absorbing what you have noticed.

▶ How words end

16. Government, environment, management, argument

The managment reserves the right to refuse admission, it says in the window of a shop near where we live. We have no wish to be admitted to a shop that is run by people who do not know how to spell *management*. But why is there an *e* there? Let us start, however, with the question of how the *government* is tackling problems of the *environment*. Too many people miss out the *n* in these words – it's not *enviroment*. This is an example of word formation – *ment* has been added to the end, so we retain the first bit – in *govern* and *environ*. But more generally, what about words like *manage*? A fairly reliable rule is that if the word ends in *e* you retain the *e* if the addition begins with a consonant (that is, *management*), but drop it if the addition begins with a vowel (that is, *managing*). But note exceptions such as *awe/awful*, *true/truly*, *due/duly*, and in particular *argue* and *argument*.

This last is worth repeating: *argument*. Many students begin the opening paragraph of their essay with the words *My arguement is*; they begin, that is, by making a small error and so immediately signal to the reader that their spelling is a possible weakness. Of course, most examiners and teachers will read straight on, but what we are highlighting here is how to avoid getting off to a poor start in an essay. Spelling key words such as *argument* correctly will give your essay-work a firm foundation because it will reflect that you have thought about what you are writing.

17. Words that end in 'ible' and 'able'

Does one add *able* or *ible* at the end of a word? Both forms of this suffix are added. *Able* is more commonly used, and is always used for words composed of other English words: *Is the water drinkable*? *Ible* is more likely to be used for some words of Latin origin: *It is barely credible that anyone could remember all these complications.* But you are respons*ible* for trying to remember, even if all the variants are not easily access*ible*. It is more often, then, *able*, but for essay purposes it is quite handy to learn the following:

> edible, eligible, fallible, feasible, flexible, forcible, indelible, intelligible, negligible, perceptible, permissible, plausible, possible, tangible, visible.

To these we can add the word *difference*, with *ence* at the end. Of course, it has nothing to do with *able* or *ible*, but like the words above it does get constantly misspelt, usually as *differance*.

18. Do words end in 'ise' or 'ize'?

At last we can generalise. Or is it generalize? The old rule used to be to use -*ize* when it relates to the Greek gela root: *organizc*, *realize*. But a much easier rule is always to use -*ise*. Perhaps the one exception is *capsize*, but all other -*ize* endings have for the most part sunk without trace (although some publishers and most Americans might take a different line).

19. Words that suffer in essays

> accommodation, commitment, definite, epitome, exaggerate, existence, fulfil (with fulfilled), harass, occur (with occurred), independent, parallel, responsible, rhythm, soliloquy.

All of these words are regularly misspelt in essays. The problem this raises is that, if you do happen to misspell one or more of them, the effect may be to lump your essay in with a lot of others. For example, students often begin an essay by writing a sentences such as *I definately disagree with the above statement*; although this may just be a slip while they are thinking through their argument, it can lead the marker to feel that the essay is going to be very similar to others beginning with similar errors. If you regularly misspell *definitely*, the best advice is try to avoid using it. You can always *disagree with this statement* without being so *definite* about it. Indeed, from a stylistic point of view it is much better to omit *definitely*. In turn, that leaves you some for manoeuvre: 'I disagree with the above statement, although there are obvious reasons why it might seem true.'

20. Is it learnt or learned, spelled or spelt?
This has to do with two aspects of language. One is that we talk about verbs being regular – that is, forming their past tense by adding *d* or *ed* to the base form (*talk* and *talked*) – and irregular, by which we mean verbs like *sleep*, which has a past tense of *slept* (this is a huge simplification, but it makes the point). Some verbs can be either, so we can have *burned* or *burnt.* The second aspect arises partly because the two spellings are close in sound:

leaned/leant

leaped/leapt

learned/learnt

Both forms are correct, but the trend is towards the *ed* ending. But *spelt* is rather more common than *spelled*, although again both are correct.

▶ Summary

We end this chapter with a brief review of what you should know about spelling. Spelling is tricky because English is such a hybrid language, but getting spelling right is something that impresses; getting it wrong can cost in examinations and more generally in life. Spelling correctly is part of studying a subject, but there are also danger areas you should watch out for:

- ▶ Key words to distinguish, especially *there* and *their*.
- ▶ Sound-alike words that have very different meanings – *were* and *where*, *to* and *too*.
- ▶ Avoidable errors – *it's* and *its*.
- ▶ Common errors – *definite*, *separate*, *argument*.

The probability is that there are, in the end, only a small number of words that you misspell frequently, and it is fairly easy to memorise these. If you spell all of the words in this chapter correctly without difficulty, you are obviously a very competent speller and already know how to watch out for the ways words appear on the page.

What you should know by now

There have been three chapters of this book so far. If we have got the tone and level of our writing right, there are a number of things you might have learnt. You might use the following as a checklist of your progress:

- ▶ How to construct a sentence.
- ▶ How to avoid comma splices.
- ▶ What subordinate clauses are.
- ▶ How to punctuate.
- ▶ How to spell common words like *their* and *its* and use them correctly.

This gives you a sound base on which to build and develop further writing skills. The next three chapters are as much to do with style as with technical competence. They offer ideas about how to avoid mangling sentences when you write in order to do your ideas justice. In a sense, if you can put together simple sentences, you can get by. Writing, however, is about more than just getting by, and in the following chapters, presented as 'Writing Confidently', we want to suggest ways in which you can improve your work.

Part Two
Writing Confidently

4 The Well-crafted Sentence

There are a lot of people who know how to construct a sentence, but who, the moment they start to write an essay, get things wrong, producing work that is marred by mistakes or by sentences that do not quite make sense. Why do things go wrong? Why do sentences sometimes read awkwardly and not convey their meaning clearly? One answer to this second question is that the writer has not thought about what he or she wants to say. Indeed, some people argue that provided you think clearly about what you are doing – about the ideas you wish to convey, the information you wish to get across, the argument you wish to develop – then the writing will take care of itself. If you bear in mind the purpose and audience of your work, they suggest, it should be the case that your writing will have direction and coherence.

There is some truth in this argument. If you have got the content of your essay under control, then it ought to be possible to present that content in a clear, logical and persuasive way. But what happens if you can't quite see your way through your ideas? Or what happens if you find writing difficult? How do you learn to write well? If we take two people, both aged twenty, why is it that one of them seems to write with ease while the other struggles with every word? Many students, it is true to say, just resign themselves to this, as if it were a fact of life, falling back on the answer that there are some people who have a natural gift for writing. And this might be the case, that some people are born to write. But all of us have the potential to transform ourselves into excellent writers. All that it requires is some thought about the process of writing, a readiness to follow the accepted rules, and a willingness not only to write but to revise and give a great deal of attention to detail. It is, we promise, worth the extra effort: if you can write well you will find that this will also enable you to think more clearly. In other words, what we are suggesting is that just as clear thinking can lead to clear writing, so sorting out your writing problems can help you sort out your ideas. The rest of this chapter is concerned with explaining how to do this, in particular by looking at the opening paragraph of an essay.

▶ Avoiding overloaded sentences

Writing is not the same as thinking out loud. There is another stage involved after thinking, in which words are sifted and selected, and then crafted and combined, in order to create a memorable impression. In this process, each sentence of an essay is both designed and built by the writer. Good sentences do not just happen: there is no such thing, in a finished essay, as an automatic flow of writing. There might be in a first draft, where you just pour out everything you know and everything you want to say, but then you have to start writing and revising in order to transform your original idea into a finished product. This is something students sometimes underestimate in terms of its importance to producing a good essay: they have put their ideas down, but have not gone through the essay again, redrafting it in order to create the best possible impression.

This has to start with the first sentence. When things go wrong in written work, they usually start to go wrong in the very first sentence. The most common mistake here is overloading: that is, trying to pack too much into one sentence. The reasons for this are fairly obvious: the student, focusing on the subject of the piece of written work and perhaps slightly anxious, starts to put down his or her thoughts, but then forgets that there comes a point at which it is necessary to pause, to conclude one sentence and begin another. The impression that is created for the reader is that the student has embarked on a sentence with no idea about where it is going to arrive; consequently, the sentence will appear to be a piece of thinking aloud rather than a crafted performance. We can illustrate this with a very simple example. This is the opening sentence of a letter. The faults in evidence, however, are characteristic of the faults that appear at the start of essays. It is a note from a parent about a child's illness:

> David was not able to attend school yesterday seeing as how the problem he is having with headaches has come back again.

There are two problems here. One is a problem about tenses, of slipping between past (*was*) and present (*is*). But the bigger problem is that the writer attempts to carry too much information in one sentence. Where it really stumbles is with the words *seeing as how*, which is an awkward transition as the writer tries to establish a bridge between two main clauses. The problem could have been avoided by stopping the sentence at an earlier point:

> David was not able to attend school yesterday. He has been having problems with headaches, and the problem has come back again.

The first sentence is kept relatively short. A second sentence has been created, but strict control is maintained here by means of the simple device of introducing the comma to create a decisive break between the two clauses in this compound sentence.

What general rules, if any, can we extrapolate from this very simple example? The main point is that we have followed the basic rules about sentence construction. We started with a simple sentence. Too many simple sentences, however, are difficult to turn into interesting prose which will hold the reader's attention and get our ideas across. We want to construct something a little more complicated than: *David was not at school yesterday. He was ill*. A string of such simple sentences would soon become wearisome, and also limit what we can say. The way forward, therefore, is to move towards more complicated sentences, but, as in our example, such sentences are constructed clause by clause and phrase by phrase. Ideas are not simply permitted to accumulate: we marshall them in line with the simple logic of sentence building. Such tight control over what we say is, paradoxically, liberating, as it is possible to say anything we want within such tight formal patterns. If we do not use them, we are likely to find ourselves relying upon tell-tale awkward phrases such as *seeing as how* to make our connections. As you start to write, therefore, remind yourself that a long, snaky introductory sentence is likely to lead to problems. Start with a simple sentence; then move to more complicated sentence structures as you expand your ideas, but ones in which you maintain control over each section or unit within the sentence.

Topic sentences

It is useful to think of the first sentence of a paragraph as the 'topic' sentence. In our revised version of the letter, the topic sentence is: *David was not able to attend school yesterday*. It is effective as an opening because it is such a controlled, almost declamatory, statement. Most essays can start in a similar way: you can create an initial dramatic and arresting effect by having a simple sentence that stands alone, not tangled up in sub-ordinate clauses and details. Look, for example, at these opening sentences from students' essays:

> Modern poetry is disturbing and problematic.

> Modern poetry, by which we mean poetry produced roughly between 1910 and 1930, falls into various categories, of which the most original is probably that referred to as 'modernist', in particular T. S. Eliot's poem *The Waste Land*.

There is nothing actually wrong with the second example here, but it does not create any great expectation that we are going to encounter an interesting essay. Rather, it is going to be an essay loaded with facts, crowded in at every comma. The first example, by contrast, is simpler, but in saying less says more, perhaps principally because the student has thought quite carefully about the construction and impact of this topic sentence.

The student who wrote that sentence has grasped an important point: you are always writing for an audience. There is something terribly dull about an essay that starts, *In this essay I will consider* . . . And even less appealing is an essay that starts, *The Oxford English Dictionary defines* . . . What you want is a topic sentence that gains the reader's attention: it can do this, however, by simply stating the issue, and then stopping before it outstays its welcome. The sentences that follow in the paragraph must then elaborate the topic. And, as your treatment of the issue gradually becomes more elaborate and expansive, the second and subsequent sentences need to become more complicated in structure, but only to the extent of introducing additional main clauses and subordinate clauses within the recognised rules of sentence composition. The point, therefore, is that your ideas cannot just be rolled out casually and conversationally. They need to be framed in sentences that obey the rules, with careful use of punctuation (that is, in particular, commas) to signal to the reader the separate units of the sentences (and so the separate units of sense). If you stick to this logic, you then have the freedom to start paying real attention to your choice of vocabulary, which will often involve sifting through various possibilities of the words that can be used. It is all a slightly more self-conscious process than you might be used to, but it is not inherently difficult; the start of a new clause, for example, is roughly equivalent to a change of gear when driving rather than a sudden change of direction.

What we are discussing in this chapter, therefore, comes back really to what we discussed in the first three chapters: write a grammatical sentence, punctuate it correctly, and make sure the individual words are working as they should. The middle section of this book is all about how to produce more confident work, but your writing can only get better if you get the basics right, if you know how to produce the right words in the right order. The way in which we want to illustrate this is by looking at a student's essay that makes the most common mistakes in a very obvious way. We discuss the first paragraph of this essay in detail, but, when it comes down to it, only one point is significant: the student is thinking out loud. The essay is a string of thoughts rather than a written performance. In the form in which the student submitted it, this could, in fact, be presented very effectively as a spoken paper in class. But it does not quite work as writing. Yet, the most minor surgery can quickly transform the essay into a good piece of written work. Indeed, this is the essence of what we are trying to say here: that, if you follow a handful of basic rules about sentence construction and punctuation, you can, within minutes, turn even a piece of work that is groaningly awful into a polished performance. And this is always the case. The problems in students' writing are always the same problems. The answer is always the same answer: **pay attention to the basic rules**.

▶ Standard errors, easy solutions

Our message, it should be apparent, is simple: the way to move forward is to go back to basics. If you want to excel as a writer, there are no fancy or elaborate tricks that have to be learnt. You merely have to become more proficient in exercising the basic skills of sentence construction. In order to drive home the points about how sentences are composed, and how important it is to be in charge of the mechanics of sentence construction and the mechanics of punctuation, we are going to examine a single essay by a student about the founding of the city of Philadelphia. At this point, you might be tempted to say that such a subject has nothing in common with the essays you have to write, but try to see that what we are discussing the whole time is how to solve problems in writing, and how solving them creates the opportunity to say more in an essay.

Here is the opening paragraph of the essay exactly as the student wrote it:

> The creation of the city of Philadelphia, and the colony of Pennsylvania at the same time, by William Penn, is often referred to as his 'Holy

Experiment'. He wanted to create a place where anyone could live, without fear. It was the first place of its kind, in America in this respect, also in the way he carefully detailed and drew up the system of government, to be implemented there, and proposal for future American colonies. In Philadelphia also, the first steps were made towards breaking away from British, and European ideas. Both in terms of thoughts and principles and appearance.

We will be discussing this in some detail, so it may help if you read it more than once. It is an interesting piece of writing, mainly because the writer has done his homework and has things to say, but it could so easily be a lot better.

First sentence

We begin by looking at the first sentence:

> The creation of the city of Philadelphia, and the colony of Pennsylvania at the same time, by William Penn, is often referred to as his 'Holy Experiment'.

Although this might appear quite a good sentence, with commas in the right places and a clear topic, there is plenty of evidence that this is, in fact, thinking out loud. The student has started with the creation of the city, then remembered the colony, and then thinks he should mention William Penn. This is typical of sentences that go awry: the student thinks of a point and writes it down, inserts a comma, then thinks of another point. Such sentences, as is the case here, are often slightly ungainly and usually read awkwardly – the information is not easily absorbed or totally clear. The sentence is also overloaded; a little too much fussy detail is being included for what should be a striking first sentence. How do we remedy the problem? We remind ourselves that the basic structure of a sentence is subject–verb–object, and we make sure that the sentence conforms a little more closely to that pattern. The subject is what William Penn created, while the verb is *referred to*. It might be a good idea, therefore, to put the subject at the start of the sentence, which is how we normally identify a subject when reading:

> William Penn's creation of the city of Philadelphia and the colony of Pennsylvania is often referred to as his 'Holy Experiment'.

We have dropped the words *at the same time*, as these words made the sentence rather too cumbersome, but if we wanted to stress this point we could start by saying *William Penn's simultaneous creation of*. Our preference, however, would be to cut even more:

> William Penn's creation of the city of Philadelphia is often referred to as his 'Holy Experiment'.

The reference to Pennsylvania, it could be argued, overloaded the topic sentence. Now, in its abbreviated and revised form, attention falls clearly on the subject and what he did. The general rule here is obvious: if you are stuck as you attempt to frame your opening sentence, resort to the subject–verb–object template which will impose a clear order and limit on what you are trying to say. Don't ramble at the outset; if at all possible, reduce what you want to say to the format of a simple sentence. Furthermore, at all subsequent points in an essay where you get stuck – that is to say, those points at which you cannot sort out your thoughts – it might well prove a good idea to fall back on a simple sentence structure, telling yourself that there must be a subject–verb–object sequence that underlies the idea you are struggling with.

Second sentence

For the moment, however, we are concerned with the opening stages of an essay. A simple topic sentence sets up the issue. Subsequent sentences must expand and elaborate upon this topic sentence, but in order to say more we will have to move beyond a one main clause simple structure. Our student wrote as his second sentence:

> He wanted to create a place where anyone could live, without fear.

Although there would be no real objection to repeating Penn's name here, the sentence quite correctly begins with the pronoun *He*. After that, however, something goes wrong. A common mistake by students is to try to make a comma do too much work, as if it can replace a few words, rather than isolate separate units of a sentence.

Just as frequently, though, a comma is inserted in a quite unnecessary way, and that initially appears to be the case here. The subject of the sentence is *He*, the verb *wanted to create*, and the object is the place and its nature. It would, therefore, be correct to write:

> He wanted to create a place where anyone could live without fear.

We suspect, however, that the writer has stumbled because he wants to suggest two points: that the place was open to all, and that people could live there without fear. It would be better if the student had produced a compound sentence, that is a sentence of two main clauses linked by a conjunction:

> He wanted to create a place where anyone could live, and live without fear.

This makes the point more clearly by expanding the idea slightly, and also adds to the overall effectiveness of the paragraph because a compound sentence now follows the simple opening sentence. The result is that the essay starts to widen out in a careful, controlled way. The student was relying on the comma to do all the work, but it was necessary to add the words *and live* to make it into a successful compound sentence.

What general rule can we extrapolate here? When a sentence is not working, check that the basic rules of sentence composition – here, how to construct a compound sentence – have been followed. It is the basic rules that provide the solution how to untangle this – and most other – sentences. If you remember this, that the basic rules will help you solve most of your writing problems, then you should be able to see how to improve almost every sentence you write.

Subsequent sentences

So far we have a topic sentence followed by a compound sentence. We need to exercise the same discipline as we advance into the rest of the paragraph. Our student, though, was not keeping to the rules, and so, as perhaps could be expected, the lack of control at the outset meant that by sentence three the writing falls apart more and more as he wrestles with his ideas:

> It was the first place of its kind, in America in this respect, also in the way he carefully detailed and drew up the system of government, to be implemented there, and proposal for future American colonies.

The student is trying to expand the reach of the essay, but stumbling in the attempt. The primary problem is again the fact that the student is thinking out loud, with the commas separating thought units rather than separating grammatical units; as such, the commas fail to contribute to the construction of meaning in the sentence, acting instead to make the writing jerky and less than clear.

We will try to sort out the problems step by step. The first main clause is:

> It was the first place of this kind, in America in this respect . . .

This sounds awkward and is wrongly punctuated. The student needs to move the phrase *in this respect* to an earlier position in the sentence to salvage it:

> It was, in this respect, the first place of its kind in America . . .

What rules have we employed here? As always, we have tried to establish the subject–verb–object sequence. But we have also had to call upon our knowledge of the punctuation rules governing commas in order to place (and punctuate) the parenthetical phrase *in this respect* in the correct manner. What we might also note about the phrase *in this respect* is that it is a nice 'enabling' touch that establishes a line of continuity and connection between the previous sentence and this sentence. In rewriting work, you should pay attention to whether the inclusion of parenthetical words and phrases (words like *however*, *therefore*, etc.) can smooth the progress and flow of your writing. Such words are a clear example of how the most minor surgery can make a considerable difference to your work.

We still, however, have to sort out the remaining problems in this student's sentence. Let's take the whole extract, but incorporating the changes we have now made:

> It was, in this respect, the first place of its kind in America, also in the way he carefully detailed and drew up the system of government, to be implemented there, and proposal for future American colonies.

The passage is still ungainly and awkward, but the more serious problem is that the rules of sentence construction are again being broken. There is a comma splice (*in America, also in the way*), where the comma is relied upon to do all the work, whereas one or two extra words – replacing *also* by *as well as* and adding a verb – would have produced a standard and effective sentence:

> It was, in this respect, the first place of its kind in America, as well as being the first in the way that Penn carefully detailed and drew up the system of government to be implemented there.

This has created a second main clause, giving us a compound sentence. We also lost an unnecessary comma towards the end. What is also apparent is that the sentence has gone on for long enough; it is better to jettison the extra fragment – *and proposal for future American colonies* – which does not make sense as it has no verb in it. Again, the student is merely thinking out loud; he is relying upon the comma to make the link rather than formulating proper grammatical units. He needs another – fresh – sentence to move the case in the paragraph forward. Instead of *and proposal for future American colonies*, we need a fresh subject–verb–object sequence, probably something on the lines of:

> These proposals served as a model for future American colonies.

Comment

The judgement we might make, after revising three of the student's sentences, is that we have to a large extent simplified and clarified matters; we have certainly simplified the pattern of the sentences, using simple sentences, compound sentences and recognising the way in which subordinate clauses can be employed. But the effect of such simplification has, in fact, been to make the essay more sophisticated because its ideas are now clear. We have identified the main clause in each sentence, but then seen what can be, or needs to be, added to it, and this has given us the precision of expression that enables the sentences to carry more weight. Instead of ideas being crowded together, each has been given a proper space to operate in:

> William Penn's creation of the city of Philadelphia is often referred to as his 'Holy Experiment'. He wanted to create a place where anyone could live, and live without fear. It was, in this respect, the first place of its kind in America, as well as being the first in the way that Penn carefully detailed and drew up the system of government to be implemented there. These proposals served as a model for future American colonies.

End of paragraph

The problems, as we have tried to make plain, are the same basic problems that appear in students' essays time after time: comma splices, fused sentences and sentence fragments. The final sentences in the student's paragraph again feature one of these errors:

> In Philadelphia also, the first steps were made towards breaking away from British, and European ideas. Both in terms of thoughts and principles, and appearance.

There are several points we can make here. First, this does not follow on all that well from the previous sentence. *In Philadelphia also* is correctly isolated by punctuation as an introductory element to the sentence, but it might be better if we used a parenthetical linking word as well. And, as we continue with the sentence, we can remove the comma after *British* as *British and European ideas* is a simple pairing, on the same lines as *cheese and onion crisps*:

> In Philadelphia, therefore, the first significant steps were made towards breaking away from British and European ideas.

Our sentence now has an introductory element, a comma, a parenthetical linking word (**therefore**), a comma, a subject (**the first significant steps**) and a verb (**were made**) followed by the rest of the sentence (the whole idea of breaking away).

The student's next sentence, however, is no more than a sentence fragment: **Both in terms of thoughts and principles and appearance**. All that is needed is a comma and a lower case **b** on **Both**, so that it becomes a phrase at the end of the sentence – **both in terms of thoughts and principles, and appearance**. But there is, in fact, another little area of muddle here, which is again common in students' essays. A fresh idea – an idea about how Penn revolutionised the appearance of American cities – has been allowed to creep into this sentence. Clear thinking leads to clear sentences. This, however, as we suggested in the introduction, also works round the other way: clear sentences would help the student sort out the cluttered nature of his ideas. If he had written a grammatical sentence rather than this fragment, he might have recognised **appearance** more closely as a fresh issue, a fresh issue that might well lead on to the next paragraph of the essay. It is an important new idea, and consequently it might be a good move to give it greater prominence in its own sentence:

> In Philadelphia, therefore, the first significant steps were made towards breaking away from British and European ideas, both in thoughts and principles. In addition to this, Penn also introduced a change in the physical appearance of a city.

This, in fact, is the only place where we have done more than tinker with the student's original draft. What the student originally wrote might have seemed pretty ramshackle, but for the most part it needed only minor adjustments to set it right. And in 99 cases out of 100 the kind of minor surgery that we have engaged in here is all that is required. Look at one of your recent essays: we are willing to bet that a little attention to the creation and continuation of the elements in each sentence, following the guidelines in this section, will solve many of the problems in it.

▶ Paragraph logic

There are only a few questions that you need to ask yourself. Have I written a sentence? Do I need a compound sentence? Do I need subordinate clauses? Have I produced all these elements in accordance with the rules? Does my sentence make sense and read well? Beyond the individual sentence, however, is the logic of a paragraph, where we need to be more aware of how each sentence as a unit combines in a larger pattern. The more we are in control of building an argument, the more we are going to be in control of the argument in an essay. This might be more apparent if we look again at the paragraph we have been discussing as the student initially wrote it and then in the revised version:

> The creation of the city of Philadelphia, and the colony of Pennsylvania at the same time, by William Penn, is often referred to as his 'Holy Experiment'. He wanted to create a place where anyone could live, without fear. It was the first place of its kind, in America in this respect, also in the way he carefully detailed and drew up the system of government, to be implemented there, and proposal for future American colonies. In Philadelphia also, the first steps were made towards breaking away from British, and European ideas. Both in terms of thoughts and principles and appearance.

In its revised version it reads:

> William Penn's creation of the city of Philadelphia is often referred to as his 'Holy Experiment'. He wanted to create a place where anyone could live, and live without fear. It was, in this respect, the first place of its kind in America, as well as being the first in the way that Penn carefully detailed and drew up the system of government to be implemented there. These proposals served as a model for future American colonies. In Philadelphia, therefore, the first significant steps were made towards breaking away from British and European ideas, both in thoughts and principles. In addition to this, Penn also introduced a change in the physical appearance of a city.

We could go through this paragraph again, polishing and perfecting the expression, perhaps, for example, not starting the last two sentences with the word *In* – the last might be changed to *Additionally* or *Moreover*.

What we are more interested in stressing here, however, is that there is a three-part structure to the paragraph. An idea is introduced in the topic sentence, which is then elaborated in the body of the paragraph; at the end, however, the paragraph arrives somewhere new, in effect creating a topic and a direction for the next paragraph of the essay. It is useful to bear in mind this idea of how a paragraph advances when you write an essay, because it helps you pay attention to how each sentence leads into, and on to, the next sentence. A paragraph that has a harmonious and coherent feel will probably always be seen to display meticulous care in the area of the negotiations between, and transition between, one sentence and the next. Nearly always it will have a clear, ordered structure that starts with a topic sentence, moves through elaborations of that topic and then arrives at a firm point ready for the next paragraph.

As an illustration of paragraph logic, look at this opening of a GCSE history essay. The person writing the essay is only sixteen, but has a firm grasp of how to construct a sentence, and how to make one sentence lead into the next. In addition, there is a clear understanding of how to present a topic sentence, and then elaborate the point, before the paragraph arrives at a point of conclusion which is, at the same time, a point of renewal.

> Absolutism is a system of government in which all social, political, cultural and spiritual activities are controlled by the king or queen. Older states were ruled by a monarch who relied upon advice from the feudal nobles. The new states in the seventeenth century, however, were ruled by kings who controlled everything. It was a form of government in which people were made totally obedient to the ruler of the state.

These are fairly straightforward sentences, though they are not simple sentences in the technical sense. They are not overloaded or excessively long. Each consists of a main clause and a subordinate clause. The ideas are developed efficiently and effectively precisely because the rules of sentence construction are adhered to. The bonus, as we have pointed out, is the three-part structure of the paragraph, moving from the topic sentence to the body of the paragraph, and then to a neat conclusion. Each sentence makes a contribution, establishing a measured and meaningful step forward.

We will return to the question of paragraphs in chapter 7, but here it is sufficient if you can see how exercising control over your sentences will almost inevitably lead to the same sort of control over your writing as a whole, but especially your paragraphs. By the same token, knowing what you are doing with your sentences and how they work will lead you towards seeing how each sentence has a role to play in the paragraph and what you wish to use it for. Writing well involves writing purposefully, but it begins with thinking not just about the content of your essay but about how you can use your writing to clarify your ideas and argument.

▶ Summary

Let's try to summarise the substance of this chapter. Look at each sentence you write and its function in the paragraph. Use simple sentences followed by complex or compound sentences, but always stick to the basic rules of grammar. Our advice about writing is, in fact, as straightforward as that. If you want to produce stunningly original work, saying the cleverest things that anyone has ever said in the history of the world, then make sure that every sentence has a subject–verb–object pattern. Second, make sure that you are in control of any extra elements that you add to, or introduce into, each sentence. It might seem a fussy business to check things like this, but it should really be as instinctive as checking certain things when driving. Even without consciously thinking about it, you need to ask yourself:

▶ Is this a sentence?
▶ Am I in control of the complications in the sentence?
▶ Have I got the right words in the right order?
▶ Does each sentence lead on from the sentence before?
▶ Do the separate sentences combine to form an effective paragraph?

5 Polished Punctuation

Points covered ▶ **Reinforcing the rules**
                        ▶ **How accurate punctuation can strengthen an essay**
                        ▶ **The colon and semicolon**
                        ▶ **Summary**

In this chapter, as in chapter 4, we continue to look closely at a student's essay. The aim is to emphasise the extent to which changes and corrections to the punctuation in an essay can improve the impact of what is being said. For the most part, everything we suggest involves very simple moves, but it is these which are too often ignored by students. Of course, if you already know how to punctuate, this could be a chapter you merely skim-read; it might prove reassuring, however, to remind yourself just how straightforward the conventions of punctuation are. And to remind yourself why the conventions are so important.

There are two dimensions to correct punctuation. First, an awareness of the rules of punctuation helps you say what you want to say, because it gives you control over your writing. You are, in effect, able to police the progress of each sentence. The second thing about correct punctuation is that, if you really know the rules, good punctuation can make your work sound weightier and more sophisticated. In particular, confident use of the semicolon can transform the quality of what you are writing. We turn to the semicolon at the end of this chapter, but in the next section we return to basics, reinforcing points we have already made about the fundamental, and essential, skills of punctuation. Notice here that we are talking about the skills rather than just the rules of punctuation. There are rules, as we have seen, about where you can and cannot put a comma, about the use of question marks and full stops. Sentences can, however, sometimes be punctuated in different ways, and this can reflect the skill or style of the writer. The differences may seem slight, but they can change the feel and flow of a paragraph. As we hope to show, these skills are not mysterious gifts but the application of the rules with a little bit of thought, often involving no more than the careful use of commas. Some writers, it has to be said, regard too many commas as fussy and distracting, while others value the clarity of meaning they can help create. Our advice, if you are in doubt, is to err on the side of including the comma – provided it is grammatically justified.

▶ Reinforcing the rules

In the last chapter, we looked at the opening paragraph of a student's essay about Philadelphia. We now want to look at some additional extracts from the same essay in order to demonstrate how a more confident awareness of the punctuation rules can add to the positive impression an essay makes by clarifying its argument and logic. In the following passage, the student is writing about a new kind of town design that was originally established in Philadelphia:

> This pattern of building new towns, can be seen to have taken off across the whole of North America. And the numbers of towns that were built as a result of the railroad, all can be seen to have taken this form. An example can be seen in Chicago, which was built under this plan, and then again in 1871, after the fire.

As in the previous extract in chapter 4, the problem here remains the way in which the student seems to be writing down thoughts in short, choppy phrases. He is not quite organising his ideas into coherent sentences. But it is again the case, as in the last chapter, that the most minor surgery – a slight degree of attention to sentence pattern, the use of commas, and word selection and order – can quickly solve the problems.

First sentence

Let's take the first sentence:

> This pattern of building new towns, can be seen to have taken off across the whole of North America.

There are two matters for discussion here. Students who are not sure about how to use commas sometimes miss them out, but just as frequently they put them in at random. The comma here, for example, is inserted almost as if the student is marking a pause while he considers how to continue with the sentence. But if we think of the subject–verb–object template, we can see that *This pattern of building new towns* is the subject, so it should not be separated by a comma from the verb *can be seen to have taken off*. That cumbersome verbal phrase is the second problem. When you are writing it is always a good idea to read what you have written back to yourself. At that point, you might realise that there is no need for such an elaborate phrase which might confuse the sentence structure. Why not just *took off*? We have, then, in the revision cut out over-elaboration and an incorrect use of a comma:

> This pattern of building new towns took off across the whole of North America.

The student could have arrived at this sentence directly if he had started from a simple subject–verb starting point. He would also have avoided putting in a comma between the subject and the verb.

Second and third sentences
The next sentences in the paragraph are:

> And the numbers of towns that were built as a result of the railroad, all can be seen to have taken this form. An example can be seen in Chicago, which was built under this plan, and then again in 1871, after the fire.

We have already touched on part of the problem here in looking at the phrase *can be seen*. There are, though, other points we can make. The first sentence is not very well structured: *all* belongs with *the towns*, and the sentence might have begun with the words *All towns*. The second sentence similarly does not read easily: it might be improved by repeating the words *was built* after *then*. This would give us:

> All the towns that were built as a result of the railroad can be seen to have taken this form. An example can be seen in Chicago, which was built under this plan, and then was built again in 1871, after the fire.

This is a little better, but we probably need to do further work to reach a more polished stage. Let's go back to the start and look at the first sentence. It begins *And*, whereas a linking phrase such as *in particular* might work better:

> In particular, the large numbers of towns that were built as a result of the railroad all took this form.

What changes have we made here? We have inserted an introductory element to the sentence, set off by a comma, but no other commas are needed after that. Then, in the process of revision, we again tried to lose superfluous or cumbersome words. You might wonder why there is no need for another comma in this sentence; it is, after all, fairly wordy. The answer is that no element of this sentence (after the introductory element) is subordinate. The subject is the enormous phrase *the towns that were built as a result of the extension of the railroad*, the verb is *took*, and the object is *this form*. So, despite its length, this is a simple sentence that, after the introductory element, does not need a comma.

The point to grasp is that we use a comma only when it is necessary, when it signals a separate unit within a sentence. It is that kind of solid hold on the basic rules that the person who wrote the essay we are looking at has not completely gained yet. The writer knows commas separate, but isn't totally sure what they separate. He is not alone in this, and it is worth repeating here the basic information:

1. We use a pair of commas, sometimes called bracketing commas, to iso-late information or an interruption to a sentence. The point about such commas is that the words they bracket could be removed and the rest would still remain a sentence. Try taking away the words *sometimes called bracketing commas* above. The remaining words are still a grammatical sentence.
2. We use commas in a list: she owns several houses, cars, companies and aeroplanes.
3. We use a comma before *and*, *or*, *but*, *yet* or *while* when these are followed by a complete sentence: *The dog barked for a day or more, but the owner did nothing about it*.
4. We do not use a comma between the subject and the verb. It is therefore wrong to write: *This pattern of building new towns, can be seen to have taken off across the whole of North America*.

Third sentence

We have already looked briefly at the sentence about Chicago:

> An example can be seen in Chicago, which was built under this plan, and then again in 1871, after the fire.

We suggested one way of revising it by repeating the verb phrase *was built* after *then*. On second thoughts, however, we think the sentence would be better if it were simplified in some way:

Chicago, for example, was built according to this plan, and then rebuilt to the same plan in 1871, after a major fire.

In the section above we played down the need for commas, but here they are essential to control the meaning. The changes we have made are as follows: we have put our initial emphasis on *Chicago*, as the subject of the sentence, and adapted *An example* to *for example*, which works as a parenthetical phrase, set off by commas, that establishes a link between the previous sentence and this one. The main clause is about how Chicago was built according to this plan, but we then have an additional main clause, marked off by a comma and the conjunction *and*. We have added a few words to make clear the idea about how it was rebuilt. Finally, we have two subordinate phrases, more precisely prepositional phrases of time: *in 1871* and *after a major fire*. Some might say that we have been too fussy in our use of commas at the end, that they are not essential for conveying the meaning to the reader, but generally in the sentence they are separating elements of the sentence and, as such, directing the reader's mind.

What general point can we extrapolate from the changes we have made in the passage? In sorting out these sentences we have got rid of any uncertainty by returning to the basic subject–verb–complement formula. This has involved omitting some words, but also, at times, adding words. Where a process of complication has proved necessary, however, we have taken extra care over how we have added phrases to, or slotted phrases into, the sentences. This has inevitably required the marking off of these elements by the use of commas, the device helping the reader grasp the pattern of a sentence, and as such, the pattern of meaning of a sentence. The point to note is that you do not use a comma just because you feel the sentence needs to pause. In this respect writing is very different from speech. In speech we communicate in information units rather than in sentences, pausing as we go. Speech thus has very different rules from writing, and it is not possible to apply the rules of one system to the other.

Final paragraph

The rules in writing are devised to serve your need to communicate clearly with your reader. They always involve the units of meaning which are the units of grammar. We can see this illustrated again if we look at the final paragraph of this student's essay, which once more needs a few changes to make it totally clear. The student has some good ideas but now needs to transform the material into a final, polished version. This is how he ends the essay:

The result therefore of William Penn's 'Holy Experiment' was the creation of a culturally diverse colony. Having an effect on the people of the rest of America for ever. The impact of Philadelphia and the region, on the whole of American life, can be seen in Penn's idea of a union. In 1697 Penn drew up a plan for a union of all the American colonies. He proposed a congress from all the colonies to deal with the common problems of war and peace. Therefore we are able to see how what started as a 'Holy Experiment' was a huge success.

We hope that you will agree that this doesn't read as easily as it might. The paragraph is not well structured, and the sequence of ideas is not fluent. A glance will tell you that the word *therefore* is repeated, as if the writer is trying to pull things together, but you cannot rely on a single word to achieve coherence. We will rewrite the passage, and then take a look at the rules we followed in order to clarify matters:

The result, therefore, of William Penn's 'Holy Experiment' was the creation of a culturally diverse colony. This also had a permanent effect on the people of America. The impact of Philadelphia and the region on American life can, in particular, be seen in Penn's idea of a union. In 1697, he drew up a plan for a union of all the American colonies, proposing a congress to deal with the common problems of war and peace. What started as a 'Holy Experiment', therefore, eventually affected the whole character of American life.

What changes and additions have we made here? There are five main ones: (1) We remembered that a parenthetical word, such as *therefore*, needs to be set off by commas; (2) we altered the sentence fragment about the effect on the rest of America, turning it into a sentence by adding a subject (*This*) and a finite verb (*had*) instead of the participle *having* which cannot act as the main verb in a sentence; (3) we then removed unnecessary commas in the sentence beginning *The impact of Philadelphia*, but added *in particular* to the sentence to establish a flow of ideas from one sentence to the next; (4) the sentence beginning *In 1697* seemed to read better when it was combined with the following sentence to form a complex sentence; (5) and finally, the last sentence had a problem that was not structural, but a matter of the choice of words. In the original version it represented a flat ending to the essay; we have tried to meet the challenge of producing a more emphatic final sentence.

We can summarise these five changes under one broad tactic: they all involve taking a step back from what was originally written, and seeing whether it can be improved. As we have tried to stress throughout, this does not mean reaching after some magical and elusive secret of good writing. All that it entails is seeing that you comply with the handful of rules about sentence construction and the placing of commas. Most of the mistakes in writing are small mistakes, where students stray from standard practice. It is just when these mistakes multiply that the problem begins to seem a big problem. Suddenly sentence after sentence goes wrong, and control slips away. But a little bit of caution in each sentence – which means obeying the simple rules – can resolve virtually all the problems in no more time than it takes to write the sentence. Indeed, if you write with the rules about sentence construction and punctuation (specifically commas) in mind, you might well find that it takes you less time to say what you want to say, because you are formulating it more quickly in coherent and effective sentences.

▶ How accurate punctuation can strengthen an essay

So far we have concentrated on how accurate punctuation can help clarify and untangle sentences. But accurate punctuation can also add to the impression of sophistication that might be conveyed by a piece of written work. The most obvious example of this is confident use of the semicolon, which, by linking what could be two separate sentences in an essay, helps draw out nuances of pattern and relationship within an argument. But the semicolon, which we deal with in the final section of this chapter, is really only an extension of the principle of combining elements to control longer sentences. We have touched on this already, but want to look more directly at the topic here.

We are going to focus on an extract from an essay on Russian history, which considers the changes that took place at the time of the Russian Revolution. The sentences in this essay are more disciplined than in the previous essay, but at times they are perhaps a little too simple. There are various places in this extract, for example, where two sentences could be linked to make the essay easier to read and sound more considered. As we have stressed, there is no secret formula involved in something like this. It is only a case of understanding the rules of sentence structure, and understanding how to use punctuation:

> At the turn of the century, Russia, both economically and politically, lagged behind the advanced industrial nations of Europe. The workers of Russia

had few rights, without trade unions. Such exploitation of the working
class caused disillusion with the existing political system. It also caused
disillusion with the existing social fabric of the nation. Added to this
working-class unrest, Russia found itself at war with Germany between
1914 and 1918. The war went badly for Russia. Government credibility was
very low. The Commander-in-Chief of the Armed Forces, the Tsar, could not
prevent defeat after defeat at the hands of Germany. Soldiers suffered from
a lack of supplies and equipment. Hostility towards the government
increased. The whole system was criticised by revolutionary groups. They
met in secret in many of the larger towns.

There is not all that much that is actually incorrect here. The student has
produced the right words in the right order. By the end, though, we might
feel that there are rather too many staccato-like sentences: each one just
seems to add a point but not to add to the argument in a lucid way. It might
also be that, throughout the paragraph, the construction of sentences
could be a touch more sophisticated.

Joining sentences

What we are trying to demonstrate is how to join sentences together to
achieve an interesting piece of work. Readers can absorb more than one
idea at a time and may feel frustrated by endless stops and starts; they are
looking for information, stimulation, thoughts and points as well as an
argument that involves them and takes them along. We should, however,
make it clear that we are not contradicting here something we said earlier.
In the first chapter we talked about the problem of the comma splice and
fused sentences. We now appear to be recommending the fusing of
sentences. What we have in mind, of course, is not fusing but instead
joining sentences in a manner that complies with all the basic rules about
sentence structure and punctuation. We will, in addition, be showing how
little phrases, such as *in addition* can establish continuity and flow in a
paragraph. Really, what we want to achieve is a paragraph where every
sentence is as impressive as the student's first sentence here:

> At the turn of the century, Russia, both economically and politically, lagged
> behind the advanced industrial nations of Europe.

That is a confident sentence. It consists of a subject–verb–object sequence
(*Russia–lagged behind–the advanced industrial nations of Europe*), but
the student also knows how to handle both the introductory element (*At
the turn of the century*) and the adverbial phrase (*both economically and
politically*).

As the paragraph continues, however, the student needs to employ such techniques a little more often. Look at the second sentence:

> The workers of Russia had few rights, without trade unions.

The word *Russia* is repeated unnecessarily, but the really awkward feature is *without trade unions* tagged on as an afterthought. It belongs in the body of the sentence:

> The workers, without trade unions, had few rights.

In addition, the next two sentences could usefully be linked with this one. To see this, we need to repeat the original four opening sentences:

> At the turn of the century, Russia, both economically and politically, lagged behind the advanced industrial nations of Europe. The workers of Russia had few rights, without trade unions. Such exploitation of the working class caused disillusion with the existing political system. It also caused disillusion with the existing social fabric of the nation.

There is, as we said, nothing wrong with these sentences, but they do seem like a list of points rather than a more co-ordinated analysis:

> The workers, without trade unions, had few rights, and the resulting exploitation of the working class caused disillusion with both the existing political system and the existing social fabric of the nation.

That isn't the only way of altering these sentences. They could be linked in other ways, or even left as they were originally, but the point we are trying to make is how compound sentences, because they are that much more expansive and wide-ranging, manage to create the impression of carrying and controlling more ideas.

This is particularly evident if we look at what to do with the sentences towards the end. There are about half-a-dozen sentences which are so straightforward and similar in structure that they sound more like notes than an essay:

> The Commander-in-Chief of the Armed Forces, the Tsar, could not prevent defeat after defeat at the hands of Germany. Soldiers suffered from a lack of supplies and equipment. Hostility towards the government increased. The whole system was criticised by revolutionary groups. They met in secret in many of the larger towns.

We can rewrite this without changing much of the vocabulary:

> The Commander-in-Chief of the Armed Forces, the Tsar, could not prevent

defeat after defeat at the hands of Germany. With soldiers suffering from a lack of supplies and equipment, hostility towards the government increased. In addition, the whole system was criticised by revolutionary groups, who met in secret in many of the larger towns.

Sentences have been carefully combined together, with a comma separating the elements, and half of each revised sentence being transformed into a subordinate clause. The effect of such a simple implementation of the rules of sentence construction and punctuation has been to create sentences that sustain two ideas rather than one. The inevitable result of this is that the paragraph conveys its information in a more interesting fashion for the reader. It also sounds more mature, as the student can be seen to be exercising more control over more material. In turn, such control suggests a more profound understanding of the implications of the points made. There is, though, no great skill or craft involved; it is only a matter of exploiting the basic rules that govern the production of a sentence.

▶ The colon and semicolon

In the last sentence of the previous section we used a semicolon rather than beginning a new sentence with 'It is only . . . '. The semicolon is probably the most sophisticated punctuation device and is, therefore, well worth adding to your repertoire. First, however, we need to establish the difference between a colon and a semicolon. As you might imagine, it is sometimes the case that in attempting to use one of these devices students opt for the wrong one.

The colon

We can dispose of the colon fairly quickly. Whereas a semicolon is like a heavy-duty comma or surrogate full stop, a colon has a more narrow role in introducing a clause or word or list that amplifies, interprets, explains or reveals what has gone before. The context in which you are most likely to encounter it, and want to use it, is essentially as a substitute for the words *as follows* or *that is*. For example:

Dickens wrote two semi-autobiographical novels: *David Copperfield* and *Great Expectations*.

The new team of four has just been announced: Short, Parker, Abbott and Cosgrove.

It is also used in the manner that we used it a couple of lines above, to introduce an indented quotation when you are writing, and also to introduce a quotation when the sentence that has preceded it can stand alone. In some contexts, where the sense continues, a comma precedes the quotation:

> When Hamlet says, 'To be, or not to be', we know that he is pondering some great question.

But if the sentence has been completed and can stand alone, a colon is used:

> Everyone knows Hamlet's famous soliloquy: 'To be, or not to be.'

These two uses of the colon are, in fact, the really straightforward ones. The first we can sum up as introducing a list of items, while the second introduces quoted material, as a stronger alternative to the comma.

Other uses of the colon have in common the idea of being an anticipatory effect, leading from what precedes to what follows. We can see it when there is a following on from one clause to another:

> I just want you to be aware of this: one false move and you're dead.

It helps you gain control of the idea of the colon if you see it very specifically as a device that moves meaning forward. In a way it is a dramatic highlighting; a statement is made, and then what follows explains or elaborates on it. Or think in terms of a simple split; the first part of the sentence makes the general point while what follows the colon is more particular or specific. Notice, however, that the colon is not followed by a dash (not thus:–, but thus:). Notice, too, the spacing: the space comes after the colon, not before or both sides of it.

The semicolon

The semicolon is a much more interesting punctuation move than the colon. It is, perhaps, for one reason above all others: it is never compulsory. It is always an extra refinement introduced into work, a subtle extra detail, and this is why it can be felt to add a touch of style to whatever you write. It is primarily used between clauses that are linked by sense but are not joined by a conjunction; each could stand as a separate sentence. That last sentence illustrates the principle. We could have written two separate sentences there, the second one starting with the word *Each*. We could have altered the sentence to:

It is primarily used between clauses that are linked by sense but are not joined by a conjunction, and each could stand as a separate sentence.

But in the version of the sentence we wrote, we elided the comma and the word *and*, so juxtaposing the sentences rather than separating them by a full stop, or joining them through the conjunction. The result is a tighter structure in which the reader gets a more compressed impression. Possibly because too much use of the word *and* to link clauses begins to sound rather naïve, the construction that involves the semicolon creates an impression of a more mature style. A sentence with a semicolon in it, slipped into a paragraph, perhaps particularly at the end, will create an impressive sense of your ability to comprehend and control more than one idea within a sentence. Partly, it has to be said, this is a matter of showing that you can employ a variety of sentence types and ways of combining them, but it also a matter of style and control; the reader sees that you are aware of how to balance sentences and ideas in a paragraph. The key points to remember, though, are:

1. The semicolon is used to join two complete sentences into a single sentence.
2. The sentences are closely related in sense or topic.

As we have noted above, if you use words such as *and* or *but* to join the sentences, you must use a comma, not a semicolon.

Some examples might illustrate how to deploy this useful weapon in your arsenal. So far in this book we have linked main clauses with a comma and a conjunction, but there are times when a semicolon might create a better impression:

His energy was unbounded, and his resourcefulness overcame every obstacle.

This could appear as:

His energy was unbounded; his resourcefulness overcame every obstacle.

An extension of this principle is where there are a number of main clauses that can be related:

There was no one part of the island better than another; it was entirely desolate and lonely; nothing lived on it but snakes and rats.

In a sentence like this we begin to see something of the logic and the effects of the semicolon. Like a comma, it creates a pause, acting rather more like a brake on the sentence, but at the same time it often carries on the reader's voice and attention from one element to the next. This sense of creating a break and yet at the same continuing and carrying forward the sense is apparent in contexts where a semicolon is used between main clauses related by *however*, *thus* or such conjunctive words:

Mary was fast approaching her sixtieth birthday; however, she had no intention of retiring.

Donald had never really grown up; therefore, it was not all that surprising to see him dressed so casually at the funeral, sporting a tattoo and ear-ring.

We also use semicolons when a sentence is long and complex and there are several main clauses, and to separate items in a series if they are too long. In these cases it is very much a matter of helping the reader to get hold of and keep tabs on the separate items in a sentence or line. The following, for example, could prove confusing:

A number of suspects had been held, including Roger Hunt, the husband of the deceased, Ruth Ellis, his wife's best friend, Jane Osborne, his former girlfriend, and Hugh Thomas, an old family friend.

In this case, the logical thing to do is to set up the list with a colon, and then separate the elements with semicolons:

A number of suspects had been held: Roger Hunt, the husband of the deceased; Ruth Ellis, his wife's best friend; Jane Osborne, his former girlfriend; and Hugh Thomas, an old family friend.

A point to remember all the time, however, is that even though the semicolon can make work sound mature, if you use it in sentence after sentence a dull, repetitive pattern of sentence structure becomes evident in your work. So, use the semicolon sparingly (and use the dash – which we deal with in chapter 8 – barely at all). Our own inclination would be, perhaps, at the most, once or twice a page, if at all, though obviously this will depend on what you want to say. But also remember that it can create the best impression at the end of a paragraph; here it can leave the reader with an impression of a control of sentence structure that echoes and reflects the control of ideas in your work.

We have acknowledged that the semicolon is optional. Some punctuation marks are not. There is never any reason for missing out a full stop, and there are lots of places where commas are absolutely required. Apostrophes are also essential. But that really clarifies the whole point about how and when to use punctuation. We need apostrophes because there will be so many occasions where the meaning of what you are trying to say will not be apparent if you don't use them accurately. There are lots of places where commas are equally essential to support meaning. But there are also occasions, particularly in short sentences, where the sentence works perfectly well even with the omission of a comma. How does one know? Well, if in doubt, err on the side of a strict interpretation of the rules. But the other way of testing this, and indeed everything in written work, is to read it back to yourself. Do the parts relate to each other and hold together? Has the reader been given enough signals? You are, after all, writing for an audience and want them to understand and be persuaded by what you write.

▶ Summary

- ▶ Use commas to bracket non-essential words or phrases in a sentence. Test by removing the words bracketed: the rest should still be a sentence. *That, we hope, is clear*. In this example, *we hope*, can easily be cut
- ▶ Use commas in a list.
- ▶ Use a comma before *and*, *or*, *but*, *yet* or *while* when these are followed by a complete sentence.
- ▶ Do not use a comma between the subject and the verb.
- ▶ Use the colon to show that what follows it explains or elaborates or identifies what is being discussed.
- ▶ Use the semicolon to join two complete sentences closely related in sense or topic into a single sentence.

6 Spelling and Usage

Points covered ▶ **Syllabilising, and pronouncing slowly**
▶ **Plurals**
▶ **The words of your subject**
▶ **Hyphens**
▶ **Frequently misspelt words**
▶ **The 'Top 30' usage tips**

In this chapter we deal again with the subject of spelling, but we also begin to move on to the broader issue of the appropriate use of words. As we have already pointed out, the rules of English spelling are at times more difficult to remember than learning the words themselves. There is the fall-back of a spell-check on a word-processor, but that should be nothing more than a final check; part of the skill involved in becoming a competent writer is making yourself more aware of words, and that includes knowing how they are spelt. What we do in this chapter is start with a few ruses that people resort to when they are unsure about the spelling of words, and then proceed to the conventions for plurals and hyphens. At the heart of the chapter is a substantial list of words that students (but not just students) frequently spell incorrectly. Then, at the end, we move on to the additional issue of the correct use of words. Often students are unsure whether they should write *could of* or *could have*, and equally unsure about the difference between *shall* and *will*. It is such matters of usage that we look at in our final section, where we try to steer a common-sense course between formal and colloquial usage.

▶ Syllabilising, and pronouncing slowly

February usually means a spell of bad weather, and bad spelling. Lots of people write *Febuary* rather than *February*. Is there a way of avoiding such an error? One helpful approach when you are unsure about a word is to sound it out very slowly to yourself, emphasising each syllable, or sound element, of the word. The result can be that the spelling of the word becomes clear, as in *Feb/ru/ary*. We can apply the same approach to words like *tem/per/at/ure* and *vet/er/in/ary* and a great many others.

Even if we do not isolate the syllables of a word, pronouncing a word slowly, carefully and with a deliberate, heavy emphasis, can sometimes help. It is not always a reliable guide, partly because so many of us elide bits of words when we speak and it is usually these bits that we misspell, but it is another aid. For example, try pronouncing these words with a heavy emphasis on each sound involved:

aspirin	irrelevant
disastrous	laboratory
environment	library
government	mischievous
history	strictly

If there are words you spell incorrectly, the fault may lie in the way you say them, so that you are caught in a circle. Some people read words backwards, trying to make them unfamiliar or they look for a pattern: we might say *asprin*, but notice that the *in* is preceded by *ir*.

Sometimes, however, the sound of words does not help at all. Particularly awkward are words that are end in *-cede*, *-ceed* and *-sede*, which all sound just the same at the end. In this case, however, there is a rule to follow, which involves remembering how to spell four words. *Supersede* ends in *-sede*, and *exceed*, *proceed* and *succeed* end in *-ceed*. All other words that might be confused with these (words such as *precede*, *concede*, *recede* and *secede*) all end in *-cede*.

▶ Plurals

A common area of confusion in spelling is the formation of plurals. This is something that is particularly important to get right because, as you can imagine, a university student who writes, for example, *sheeps* appears very silly. There is, of course, no *argument* about that (note, again, that there is no *e* in the middle of the word, it is *argument*, not *arguement*). Most nouns form plurals just by adding *-s* to the singular form:

boy, boys   chair, chairs

girl, girls   Sunday, Sundays

But a number of nouns ending in *f* or *fe* form the plural by changing the ending to *ve* before adding the -*s*.

leaf, leaves   wife, wives

knife, knives   yourself, yourselves

Singular nouns ending in -*s*, *sh*, -*ch* or -*x* form the plural by adding -*es*:

kiss, kisses   church, churches

fish, fishes   tax, taxes

All of these are fairly straightforward. Where we are more likely to make mistakes is with words ending in -*o*. If the *o* is preceded by a vowel, it is usually a case of just adding -*s* (*radio*, *radios*; *zoo*, *zoos*). But if the *o* is preceded by a consonant, the plural form is usually -*es* (*hero*, *heroes*; *tomato*, *tomatoes*). We could go on to elaborate more rules, but the fact is that, in the end, you simply have to know in most cases, and then check if you are unsure. This is probably where most students go wrong. It is the old saying about spoiling the ship for a ha'porth of tar. We often encounter essays where students have worked for days on what they have written, but then at the last moment have failed to spend half an hour going through and checking every aspect of the presentation and spelling. This is misguided: the marker cannot focus exclusively on your ideas, and a poorly spelt and punctuated piece of work is bound to do less well than one with few errors.

There are cases where plural spellings seem to be controversial. Some people will accept only *curricula* as the plural of *curriculum*, while others will use *curriculums*. Then there are American spellings: Britain favours *programme* for the listing of television shows, but uses *program* (the American spelling) for anything to do with computers. The verb form, though, is *programmed*. And there are words such as *color*, *flavor* and *center*, which are American English spellings that could confuse the unwary: British English has *colour*, *flavour* and *centre*.

▶ **The words of your subject**

The issue of taking care and checking is particularly important in relation to the words that are used in your subject over and over again. It is absolutely vital that you spell correctly the names of the authors, texts and topics that you refer to in an essay. If the name of a character in a novel is *Marlow*, and you write his name as *Marlowe*, you are inadvertently confusing him with Shakespeare's rival playwright. Similarly, if you are studying *Wuthering Heights*, you ought to spot that the name of the principal character is *Heathcliff*, not *Heathcliffe*, with an *e* on the end. Errors of this kind, though seemingly small, can undermine the authority of your work. You must, then, make totally sure that you have checked the spelling of authors' names, the names of texts, and the names of characters, places, concepts and issues referred to in books.

This applies in every subject: there are geography essays written about the *environment* and *environmental issues* by students who are unaware that there is an *n* in the middle of the word. Similarly, politics students have been known to spell *government* without its middle *n*. The list continues: literature students must know how to spell the word *tragedy*; history students should know the difference between *the nineteenth century* and *nineteenth-century Britain*, and why there is a hyphen in the second case; lots of medical students (and doctors) do not know how to spell *influenza*. And there are plenty of maths students who prefer to stick to *maths* rather than *mathematics*.

Of course, this list is, in part, anecdotal: we have not had time to check every script in every subject in Britain for the commonest errors. What we are saying is, know the words used in your subject and spell them correctly. More particularly, make sure that you spell correctly any word used in the question that has been set. If you really cannot decide how a word is spelt, use a different word. But always, if in doubt, you should consult a dictionary.

▶ **Hyphens**

Spelling is largely a matter of paying attention and taking care. There are, however, a few areas where even the most confident speller can feel a little uncertain. The most frequent example of this is when two words are combined, as in, say *gamekeeper*. Why do we sometimes use a hyphenated word and sometimes, as with gamekeeper, amalgamate what are clearly two separate words into one word? There are, in fact, two aspects to this issue of hyphens: words that function on their own, and words that acquire a hyphen because they are being used as an adjectival phrase. Let's deal with the latter first. Look at these two sentences:

In the nineteenth century, Britain became an industrial nation.

Nineteenth-century Britain saw the rapid rise of industry.

Why, you might well ask, does the second sentence have a hyphen in *nineteenth-century* whereas an apparently identical structure in the first sentence does not? But the two structures are not identical. In the first sentence *nineteenth* is an adjective and *century* is a noun; they have, therefore, different grammatical functions. In the second sentence, *Britain* is still the noun in this portion of the sentence, but *nineteenth* and *century* together form a compound adjective qualifying *Britain*, and so are hyphenated. Although it is clear what is meant by *nineteenth century Britain* without the hyphen, elsewhere there is room for confusion. Look at this:

He swallowed six inch nails.

That sentence means that he swallowed six nails, all of which were an inch long. If we wanted to suggest that he swallowed long nails, we would write:

He swallowed six-inch nails.

If the distinction is still not clear, think about what this sentence might mean:

The donkeys on the beach all appeared to have twelve inch ears.

A hyphen might help make the impression less bizarre, and more accurate.

What we have dealt with so far is adjectives formed from two or more words. Other examples of use of the hyphen include fractions (*two-thirds*, *three-quarters*), the quarters of the compass (*north-east* and so on), and most words that begin with a prefix such as *ex*, *anti*, *non* and *neo*. Thus we write *anti-fascist*, *non-existent*, *neo-Nazi*. Also, we usually use a hyphen for separating identical letters. We would, therefore, write *book-keeping*, *co-operate*, *pre-eminent*, *pre-empt*. But this only applies if it is separating identical letters, so it is *re-entry* but *rearrange*. It has, however, to be admitted that most people now write *cooperative*, so that is an example of a convention changing under usage. The same seems to have happened with words such as *override* and *overrule* , *withhold* and *underrate*. We still use the hyphen in nouns formed from prepositional verbs such as *build-up*, *call-up* and *set-up*.

A vaguer area is when two words become one. A person might show *common sense*, which would make him or her a person with *commonsense* views. The adjectival phrase here has become one word. The explanation would seem to be frequency of usage. As with *semicolon*, when we use a phrase over and over again, usage has tended to convert it into one word. But there are also words that used to require two hyphens where these have all but disappeared. You will find both my *brother-in-law* and *brother in law*, and *prisoners-of-war* and *prisoners of war*. Although generalisations are always flawed, the pattern seems to be to turn hyphenated words into compounds once they are established (*the word-processor* becoming *the wordprocessor*), or to drop the hyphens once everybody knows what is meant (*the word processor*). At some stages, as with this last example, there are several variant spellings in use.

▶ Frequently misspelt words

There are, as you can see, a great many little conventions that have to be absorbed, but the thing about something like the use of hyphens is that there is some logic involved; they are just a matter of common sense. The rule followed is that you make sure the graphic presentation of your work (that is, putting in the hyphens) makes your meaning clear to your reader. But there are no such rules for a whole mass of tricky words. The best tip here is to start compiling your own spelling list. Most people have a small set of words that they misspell time and time again. And when they are studying a certain subject at university it becomes all the easier to identify the words that crop up in the subject and in their essays, and which are repeatedly spelt incorrectly. The majority of us, when it comes down to it, have about 25–50 words that we need to notice the spelling of. The best way of tackling this problem is to have a piece of paper on your desk or notice-board on which you list the words you have been getting wrong. We know this is boring and rather patronising advice, but the point is that it works.

Many of the perfectly ordinary, run-of-the-mill words you might have problems with may appear in the list on page 87, which contains words that students repeatedly get wrong.

▶ The 'Top 30' usage tips

There are numerous things that can go wrong when you are writing, ranging from the isolated word that is spelt incorrectly to an entire

Frequently misspelt words

1	absence	34	experience	67	prejudice
2	across	35	extremely	68	privilege
3	accommodate	36	familiar	69	probably
4	acknowledge	37	foreign	70	psychology
5	actually	38	government	71	receipt
6	all right	39	guarantee	72	receive
7	amateur	40	guard	73	recommend
8	analyse	41	height	74	reference
9	appearance	42	humorous	75	relieve
10	appreciate	43	immediately	76	religious
11	argument	44	independent	77	repetition
12	awkward	45	intelligence	78	rhythm
13	beginning	46	interest	79	ridiculous
14	belief	47	knowledge	80	sacrifice
15	business	48	laboratory	81	scene
16	committee	49	length	82	schedule
17	criticism	50	library	83	secretary
18	definitely	51	lying	84	separate
19	dependent	52	meant	85	severely
20	difference	53	neither	86	similar
21	disastrous	54	ninety	88	sincerely
22	discipline	55	nuclear	89	straight
23	discussed	56	occasionally	90	succeed
24	disease	57	opinion	91	success
25	dysfunctional	58	opportunity	92	surprise
26	eighth	59	parallel	93	thoroughly
27	eligible	60	particular	94	though
28	eliminate	61	persuade	95	tragedy
29	embarrassed	62	physically	96	unfortunately
30	environment	63	pleasant	97	unnecessary
31	especially	64	possible	98	until
32	exaggerate	65	practical	99	unusual
33	excellent	66	preferred	100	usually

sentence that fails to make sense. Some of the most common problems, however, are problems of usage, of being unclear about, for example, the difference between *flaunt* and *flout*, or whether *hanged* or *hung* is correct (see below). Writing is all about paying attention to detail, which means making sure that you always get the right words in the right order. But if you do not know the conventions of usage, you are almost bound to come unstuck. We have, therefore, listed below, in alphabetical order, a 'Top 30' of the niggling little queries about usage.

1. Agree to, agree with

Agree to means that you accept what someone proposes (although you might, of course, *agree to differ*). *Agree with* means that one person or thing is in accord with another: *I agree to that suggestion*; *I agree with you about the need for more trees*.

2. All right

All right is two words, and means that everything is correct: *The spellings were all right*. *Alright* is used to mean 'well', 'unhurt': *The student was alright after the crash*. The two are commonly confused. Some dictionaries do not recognise 'alright' as a word. In formal writing, use *all right*.

3. All together, altogether

All together means gathered in one place or in union, whereas *altogether* means entirely or totally, with nothing left out: *At last the family were all together*; *altogether, it had been a night to remember*.

4. Among, between

Among is used when more than two are involved. *Between* involves only two. *Between you and me, I'd rather not be among my relatives at Christmas*. The distinction between *among* and *amongst* also causes some confusion. Essentially, there is no difference of meaning, so choose whichever you prefer. It is worth remembering, however, that *among* is used far more often, and possibly more often with every year that passes.

Why, however, should we say *between you and me* rather than *between you and I*? Think in terms of a parallel: *it's between you and them*, not *it's between you and they*. Prepositions such as *to*, *for after* and *from*, like *between*, are all followed by the *me* form. What this in effect means is that *me* here is acting as an object, not as the subject. The same would be true of *us*, *him*, *her* and *them*, which are the objective form of the personal pronouns *we*, *he*, *she* and *they*.

5. Are, is

Be quite sure to remember to use *are* with a plural subject, and *is* with a singular subject. You would write *the man is*, but *the men are*. Sometimes, however, you have to check that you are making a connection with the true subject of the sentence. You should write *The number of men is falling* because the *is* agrees with the singular noun *number*, not with the plural word *men*, although the practice is often different in speech. The convention for bracketed extensions is that the verb agrees with the subject before the bracket: *My sister (and most women of her age) is*.

Another problem area arises with nouns such as 'family' and 'government' where either *is* or *are* is acceptable nowadays according to modern linguists. Traditionalists still prefer to treat these collective nouns as singular: *the committee is still meeting*. Using the plural, however, is not wrong: *the team have played well*.

6. As, like
He attended church on Sunday, like he always had. A sentence such as that in an essay might sound better if *as* were substituted for *like*: *He attended church on Sunday, as he always had*. *Like* is acceptable, but informal (*If you knew Suzie, like I know Suzie*), and is seen as more colloquial by association (*like wot he 'ad always done*). It is, then, advisable to stick to *as* when writing. *Like* is reserved for resemblance: *I had never met anyone like Suzie*.

7. Assure, ensure, insure
I can promise you, or assure you, that I have made certain, or ensured, that we are protected with a sound insurance policy. *Ensure* and *insure* are often used interchangeably to mean 'make certain', but *insure* is restricted to legal and financial protection. You therefore *insure* your property against burglary; you *ensure* that your house is locked up before you go out by checking all the doors and windows. *Assure* means to promise or guarantee: *I assure you we will pay for the damage*.

8. But, however, yet
Each of these words expresses contrast. *But* can be used to begin a sentence (just don't use it to start too many sentences). *However* is virtually interchangeable with *but*, and can be used in different positions to give stylistic variation in an essay: *It is, however, up to you; However, it is up to you*. *Yet* suggests continuity rather than an absolute contrast: *The monarchy is outmoded, yet it survives*. But notice the important difference when we use *but* to join two main clauses:

It is up to you, but I am not going.

It is up to you; however, I am not going.

9. Different from, different than

Different from is the most acceptable form, but *than* will often be used after *differently*: *They do things differently these days than when I was a girl*. But *from* could be used here, so if in doubt, stick to *different from*. *Different to* is also used increasingly instead of *different from* and may be the preferred form soon. At the moment, however, *different from* is the safest to use.

10. Disinterested, uninterested

Judges should be *disinterested*, that is, they should not take sides, but if they are *uninterested* there is cause for concern, because they are bored stiff by the case. *Disinterested* means impartial; *uninterested* means bored. However, this is another case where usage is forcing a change slowly, so that *disinterested* is more and more being used to mean 'uninterested'. In turn this means that the impartial meaning of 'disinterested' is disappearing. Perhaps nobody is interested any more.

11. Due to, owing to

Owing to means 'because of'; *due to* means 'caused by' and is always correct after it follows a form of the verb 'to be': *Her grey hairs were due to worry*, but *Owing to the snow, the train was cancelled*.

A clear rule is to use *due to* after the verb 'to be' and either form elsewhere. But to repeat: *He was late owing to traffic* is correct; *his lateness was due to traffic* is correct, but the common *He was late due to traffic* is wrong even though it sounds right (substitute 'caused by' here for 'due to' and you'll get the point).

12. Farther, further

In a narrow sense, *farther* refers to additional distance, and *further* to additional time, amount or abstract matters. But *further* is now often used for both time and distance. *Farther*, however, can only be used for distance, so you could say *Is it much further, father?*, or *Is it much farther, father?* The simplest solution is to use only *further*.

13. Flaunt, flout

Try to avoid mixing these up: *flaunting* is showing off, whereas *flouting* is defying convention. We do not *flaunt authority* but *flout* or defy it; you *flout* a decision, but *flaunt* your wealth, as if in contempt of others.

14. Hanged, hung
You *hang* a picture and *hang* a prisoner, but if you did it yesterday you *hung* a picture and *hanged* a person. *Hanged* is used for executions, therefore, but *hung* for all other meanings.

15. Have, of
Be careful that you use *have* after 'helping' or 'auxiliary' verbs. The ones to watch out for are *could*, *should*, *may* and *might*. Make sure that you write *could have*, *should have*, *would have*, *may have* and *might have*.

The following are always wrong: *could of, should of, would of, may of, might of*.

16. Imply, infer
Another pair of words that are sometimes muddled in essays. *Imply* means suggest; *infer* means conclude or deduce something from something: *I infer from your actions that you are guilty*; *you imply that I am lying*. A writer or speaker or text, then, *implies* something, but readers *infer* what is meant. Only people can *infer*; a text might *imply* something, but it cannot infer.

17. In, into
In indicates location or condition: *she was in the house*. *Into* indicates movement or a change of condition: *she went into the garage*. Here *into* is one word because it is followed by a noun, *garage*. When a verb comes next, the *to* is part of the verb and so *into* is two words, *in to*. Thus, *she went in to find a saw*.

A similar pair is *on* and *onto*: *on* is used as an adverb (*let's move on to the next subject*), whereas *onto* is used as a compound preposition (*she jumped onto the horse*). The simple rule is that *on to* is always two words when it is impossible to use just *on* alone: *pass this on to the next person*.

18. Later, latter
Latter is the second-named of two items, former the first. *Later* refers to time: *Henry and George decided to leave. 'See you later,' said the latter*.

19. Like, such as
Like suggests resemblance and means 'similar to': thus *a band like Oasis*

means a band that resembles them, but it also nowadays means 'a band such as Oasis'. In other words, *like* has come to have two meanings where previously there was a clear distinction between 'like' and 'such as'. *Such as* is used to precede an example or examples of a larger subject: *there are great bands such as Oasis and Radiohead*. Bands here is the larger generic term, while the named bands are individual examples of bands.

20. May be, maybe

If you are unsure which to use, ask yourself whether the word *perhaps* could be used as a substitute. If it can, the word required is *maybe*. *Maybe* is an adverb meaning *perhaps*. *May be* is a verb group used thus: *it may be right, or it may be wrong*.

21. Media

Media is the plural of *medium*. There are two things to be on guard about. You should write *television is the most important medium in society* (not *media*). When you use the plural *media*, you require *are* rather than *is* after it: *The media are to be congratulated for exposing Tory sleaze*. There is a word *mediums*: this is the plural of the word 'medium', meaning a spiritualist or person claiming to be in contact with the spirits of the dead.

22. On, upon

On will always do; you don't need to use *upon* unless you think it sounds more formal in a particular sentence.

23. Shall, will

Will is gradually displacing *shall*. In common usage, *will* is the future time helping verb for all persons: *I will be leaving tomorrow*.

The conventional rule is that *I* and *we* take *shall* for the future – *I/we shall be leaving tomorrow* – and that *you/he/she/it* take *will*: *he will be going today*. And then, secondly, that we reverse these when we wish to express intention or determination: *we will get there*; *you shall do as you are told*.

Use whichever sounds best to you, but you aren't going to go wrong with *will*. *Shall* is mainly used in first-person questions requesting an opinion or consent: *Shall I order a takeaway tonight? Shall we dance?* But you would write *When will I see you again?* Because *shall* has a slightly dated, formal air, it can be used when a formal effect is required: *I shall do it; I'm determined to succeed*.

24. Should, would

Should expresses obligation or perhaps moral duty, whereas *would* expresses a wish or hypothetical condition. *I should visit my aunt, and I would if I could be bothered*. *Should* these days, therefore, is used mainly as a synonym for *ought to*.

25. That, which

There are several points here. First, *that* is often regarded as an informal equivalent of both *who* and *which*, and used in speech in place of either. Second, *who* is used for people: *the women who won*; *which* is used for animals and things: *the boat which sank*; *that* is also used for animals and things. Third, there are two uses of *which*, only one of which requires commas:

> The pictures, which are due back tomorrow, are very clear.

> The pictures which have been sent back are very clear.

The difference here is that, in the second example, the information *which have been sent back* is essential to identify what is being talked about and so is not separated off by commas. In the second example we could substitute *that* for *which*, but not in the first: *that* cannot be used for what are called non-restrictive clauses.

It is, then, a reasonable rule of thumb to stick to *which* after a comma. *The school that I attended* and *the school which I attended* are both acceptable, but *the school, which is in Middlesex, has now been demolished* illustrates how *which* follows a comma.

26. Till, until

Till and *until* have the same meaning, and either can be used. *Until* is the more formal word, and is the preferred choice at the start of a sentence.

27. Toward, towards

The words are interchangeable. *Towards* is preferred in Britain, and *toward* in America. Choose which form you are going to use, and stick with it; don't slip from one to the other.

28. Which, who

Which never refers to people. *Who*, or sometimes *that*, is used for people: usually *that* refers to persons when they are anonymous or a group: *the children that came here*. But *the children who came here* is also correct.

29. Who's, whose

Who's is a contraction of *who is* or *who has*. *Whose* is a possessive. *Who's there? Who's been eating my porridge? Whose car is making that noise?* If you confuse these two, a straightforward answer is never to write *who's* but to stick to *who is*. Or, if you do write it, make sure you translate it in your head as 'who is'. The same applies to all contractions.

30. Your, you're

You're is a contraction of *you are*. *Your* is a possessive. *You're a big baby. Your baby is asleep*. Once again, it is perhaps better to avoid *you're* in any formal work if you are likely to confuse it with *your*. It would be just as easy to write *You are a big baby*.

Still confused? Or possibly more confused than ever? The niggles we have listed here will not destroy an essay. The ones you need to sort out and be sure of are 5, 15, 16, 20, 29 and 30. The rest are a bonus which will put you in front of the field. We could add other pairs of words that will help you sharpen your grasp. There is, for example, the difference between *less* and *fewer*, *bought* and *brought*, *allusion* and *illusion*, but the only real advice we have to offer is the standard advice: once you have written it, check it; if you are still unsure, find another word or structure the sentence in a different way to get round the problem.

Part Three
Writing with Style

7 Writing an Essay

Writing an essay is a complex performance. What always surprises us is not the fact that so many people make mistakes, but that so many people make such a good job of it. Every paragraph of an essay involves perhaps a hundred conscious or half-conscious decisions about what word to use, how to structure and punctuate a sentence, and how to organise and present one's work. Each paragraph of an essay is essentially an elaborate piece of architecture that the writer has had both to design and build. Examiners are, therefore, going to be reasonably tolerant if a few elements in the overall structure are a little shaky.

The building metaphor for constructing an essay is a useful one as it helps us see that there is a logic, a design principle, that informs the activity. It is this that we concentrate on in this chapter. So far we have focused mainly on the skills involved in building a sentence and how to ensure your work is technically correct; we're now going to move on to how to build an essay, including how to shape a paragraph and a sentence. It might seem odd to deal with the larger concern, the essay, first and then the smaller units of the paragraph and sentence, since when we write we obviously go from sentence to paragraph to essay. What we are concerned with, however, is how all the parts fit together and how to know what you are doing will help produce a successful essay. There are some techniques involved that can easily be learned and which make the whole project of writing an essay an interesting challenge rather than a prospect to be dreaded.

▶ Constructing an essay

General principles

Writing an essay requires planning and organisation. It is not enough to look at the question, and then start writing your answer. You need to think about the wording of the question: most questions pose a problem of some sort which you have to debate. The key words here are *Discuss*, *Account for*, *How far*, words that signal you need to provide evidence and analyse the material. You also need to plan your answer so that you don't simply put down some loose thoughts as a way of starting. It's much better to spend some time generating your ideas and then organising them into an essay rather than pouring out everything you know. You need, then, to think about the shape, and even rhythm, of your answer.

This, however, is the kind of general, perhaps not always very helpful, advice that people will offer to you over and over again. So let's be rather more specific. One of the most useful rules in writing an essay, indeed possibly the best tip of all, is the 'rule of three'. It is a rule that can be made use of in constructing an essay as a whole, in constructing a paragraph, and even in relation to constructing a sentence. We explain and expand the 'rule' in the course of this chapter, but, in a sense, you already know it. Everybody knows that an essay needs a beginning, a middle and an end; they know, that is, that an essay basically has three parts, and that these three parts are not all the same length. The meat of the essay lies in the middle, and it is here that all the problems lie. How do you organise it so that it works? And how can knowing the shape of your essay help you with the content?

Let's start with some general principles. If we consider a scientific experiment, it will probably follow a standard format. The experiment starts with certain materials and a number of expectations; we then conduct the experiment; and, if the experiment has worked successfully, we arrive somewhere new. We have advanced our knowledge. For example, scientists were curious about the qualities of, and applications of, bacteria; they studied the formation of bacteria in their experiments; and the end result was, in one case, the development of antibiotics, in particular penicillin. What happens in this, or any experiment, is that the project is set up, then moved along, until it eventually arrives somewhere. Now, if we wanted to write a scientific report on an experiment, how would we go about presenting it? We might choose to write three very long paragraphs, with a paragraph for each of the three steps we have described. That would give us a sort of essay shape, but without any clear beginning or end. It might be better to have eight paragraphs: one to introduce the topic, two to describe the materials and expectations, two to describe the method of the experiment, and two for the results and conclusions, before a final short paragraph summing everything up. In other words, what we can do is divide the middle section, the core of the essay, into three well-defined stages. The basic shape is still beginning, middle and end, but now there is a real structure for the main part of the essay. The advantage of a structure like this is that we have moved through the materials sequentially – keeping an order of three stages – but we have also thought in terms of a clear and persuasive essay format that a reader can follow.

Rule of three

Such a method seems to be readily applicable to a scientific experiment where there is usually a set order for doing things, but is it going to have any relevance for an essay on, say, the life of Florence Nightingale? We think it is again a good idea to think in terms of a rule of three. The temptation in writing about someone's life in a history essay might be just to produce an endless list on the lines of she did this, then she did this, and then she did this. But if we divide the core of essay into three stages we start to impose a shape on the raw material; we begin to think in terms of an argument, of setting the issue up, pushing the issue along, and then seeing where we arrive. The essay immediately begins to acquire some shape and direction, and this is true even before we have considered what we are going to include in each section of the essay. In an essay on Florence Nightingale, we could follow the eight-paragraph format we described above. An introductory paragraph might give a very brief outline of her life. The first stage of the essay (paragraphs two and three) could describe the context in which she grew up and what was expected of a woman of her class; the middle stage of the essay (paragraphs four and five) could describe her well-known achievements as a nurse and administrator of nursing in the Crimean War; and then the last section of the essay (paragraphs six and seven) could consider the consequences – for Nightingale herself, for the profession of nursing, and more generally for women as people with an active contribution to make in society. It might choose to explain this through an examination of Nightingale's career in the years following the Crimean War. A final paragraph, of perhaps no more than ten lines, would then provide you with an opportunity to sum up the significance of the material, themes and issues you have presented.

The same structure – set the issue up, move it along, see where you arrive – will work for virtually any essay set on any subject at university.

The attraction of such a structure is that it avoids the most frequent shortcomings in students' essay writing. Far too often students produce shapeless essays, in which they ramble through or around the alleged subject of their essays with very little idea where they are going. What such essays lack is a disciplined structure and sense of direction. It is possible to devise other essay formats and schemes, but they tend to be too specific to one subject or one issue. For example, language students might be asked to report on the five main aspects of language in a passage rather than to develop an essay on it; in creative writing, you might be asked to come up with as many ideas as possible and then to review and assess these. These are different kinds of writing exercise with their own logic, and can be adopted for formal, academic work. The great advantage of the rule of three essay method, however, is that it works on the lines of the general logic of all argument – that you introduce your propositions, develop them and draw conclusions. Or we would put that even more simply and say that the great advantage of a rule of three essay method is that it ensures that an essay has a beginning, a middle and an end both in the literal sense and in terms of its central argument built in three stages. It guards, therefore, against the directionless essay, or the essay that loses its sense of direction.

In a standard undergraduate essay at university (an essay that is generally somewhere between 1500 and 2000 words), it is, we believe, a good idea, at least to begin with and until you have found your writing feet, to think in terms of producing eight paragraphs. Start with a short opening paragraph and finish with a short closing paragraph, perhaps of no more than ten lines each. Avoid spending all your time on the introduction and then unnecessarily repeating points in the conclusion. It is usually a danger sign in an essay if the opening paragraph is too long, for what it means is that you have overloaded the opening of your essay with more material than you need or can control at that stage. An essay is always written for an audience, and a long opening paragraph will lose and confuse your reader (and probably lose and confuse you as the person writing the essay). The closing paragraph should be equally short and to the point, for its only function is to draw the threads together of what you have established in your essay.

In between the opening and closing paragraphs, we recommend that you aim for six paragraphs that are fairly substantial and also fairly equal in length: about one-half to two-thirds of a page. Paragraphs that are much longer than this will tend to lose the thread of what you are trying to say. Short paragraphs – paragraphs, in particular, of no more than four or five lines – should be a real warning signal to you that something is going wrong in the writing of an essay, for short paragraphs are making bitty little observations that float on their own rather than contributing to the steady overall step-by-step development of the essay.

It might be objected that this advice sells essay writing short; that in real life people write very short paragraphs and very long paragraphs; that length has nothing to do with an essay and that what matters are ideas. Shouldn't an essay be driven by its content, not by its form? If you have nine ideas, how can you fit them into this format? Isn't the best way to make a list of points, get them into a skeleton order, write your topic sentence for each paragraph and then summarise the essay in the opening paragraph? Certainly this is a valid approach, and we know a lot of students prefer to tackle essay-writing in this way. But we also know a huge number of students who cannot get any kind of argument going in their essay or see how to make it work. If that is your position, then you have nothing to lose by adopting the eight-paragraph format. Indeed, you have everything to gain.

Longer essays

The six paragraphs that constitute the central body of your essay work best if you very consciously tell yourself that you are dividing your thinking into the three steps of introducing the topic, advancing the logic and finally arriving somewhere. It often takes students a long time to see that nearly all the best essays – and a great many of the books and articles they are encouraged to read – are simple in structure in this kind of way. This, however, is part of the whole ethos of studying a subject at university. There are lots of people who can never see the wood for the trees. In essay writing they might spend all their time on making sure they get every point in, but never manage to see the overall shape of what they should be aiming for in an essay. And such people adopt a similar attitude to their subject: they make endless notes in lectures, in a sense noticing and recording every tree, but they don't grasp the larger picture, the thread that connects every lecture, and which constitutes the essence of the subject they are studying. You need to discover the broad pattern in your subject; in the same way, you need to spot the broad pattern in essay writing. If you get the broad pattern right, it will provide the structure in which all the details can find a place.

In essay writing, as we have suggested, a simple three-stage sequence will look after the essay's shape and progress. You can then put your effort into what really matters, into the details of the argument. You have taken care of the grand shape (in fact, the essay structure automatically takes care of the overall progress of the essay), so you can focus on getting the content of each paragraph right. We have suggested an eight-paragraph structure, but with a longer essay you might decide to have more paragraphs in each stage. An essay of 2,500 words, for example, would suggest an essay structure of eleven paragraphs: an introductory paragraph, the three steps to the essay with three paragraphs in each section, and a conclusion. An essay of 5000 words might divide into an introduction, three sections each consisting of six paragraphs, and a conclusion; that is to say, you would know before you even started writing it that your 5000 word essay was going to have twenty paragraphs. And you would be as clear as you were with an eight-paragraph essay that it was going to move through three steps or stages. The essence of much of what we are saying is that it is unwise to start with the essay title and then to try to discover the form of your essay. The form and substance of your essay can be decided before you even see or select the title; if you do this, it not only saves you an immense amount of work – as the whole shape and direction of your answer is already worked out – but, in addition, it virtually guarantees that you will produce a better essay.

It is again worth airing some of the objections you might have to this. You might feel that what we have suggested will work well enough if you know the topic, but that for research assignments other procedures are needed. In some cases it might seem better to explore your ideas in a loose, draft form, and then to redraft and think it all through again. A lot of people, we know, like to work in this way. Often, though, what they are aiming for is exactly what we have set out above: a controlled piece of writing that builds an argument in stages. In a sense, what we are suggesting is to cut back on the preliminary drafting and get on with the producing of the essay in a form that will lend itself much more readily to revision and polishing. Rough drafts can be helpful, but they can also be a nightmare of notes, ideas and points. All teachers have been faced by the student who brings in a 'rough draft' of ten pages of scribbled handwriting in a mixture of pen and pencil, with diagrams, plans and booklist. The advice we give is always the same: eight (or eleven or twenty) paragraphs will see you through.

Examples

We have demonstrated how we would apply this method to an essay on Florence Nightingale, but can it really be said to apply anywhere, and to any subject? Well, one thing you might wish to consider is that in a timed situation you have to produce an essay that demonstrates not only your reading and thinking but also your writing skills. Of course, most examiners make tremendous allowances for work done under pressure and don't expect a perfect performance, but a student who can turn in a measured, controlled piece of writing always impresses in examinations. The same applies, curiously, to word-processed essays. These are usually very professional in appearance, but what matters is the weight of the argument and how that is executed from beginning to end.

But let's look at how the advice applies in other areas. If you were studying politics, or taking a general studies paper, you might have to write an essay about the victory of the Labour Party in the 1997 General Election, and the humiliation of the Conservative Party in that election. In an unplanned essay, you might start by saying that Labour had been out of office for eighteen years, then wander on to the part that Tony Blair played, perhaps touching on the divisions within the Conservative Party. But it would be a loose collection of ideas in which you were looking for a shape and direction. It seems to make a lot more sense to establish some opening propositions, then to see what happened next, and finally to consider what this led to. After an opening paragraph outlining the bare facts, therefore, you might start with the position before the election (Tony Blair reforming the Labour Party, and divisions over Europe in the Conservative Party), then go on to the actual campaign (how the campaign went for both main parties), and then the result (where you might try to analyse the significance that can be read into the result).

The point is that within such a three-step sequence you have total control of the argument and the material you want to include in the argument. We once saw a television programme about a broadcaster who had spent his entire life working for the BBC. He had always been very popular and successful, but openly admitted that in every interview he had conducted on television he had only ever asked three questions: 'How did all this come about?', 'What happened next?', 'And then?' The fact is that most academic essays can ultimately be reduced to this simple format, and will almost inevitably work better if they are reduced to this format.

There are, though, a few more tricks involved in essay writing, in particular, how to start and how to finish. In opening an essay the secret is not to fall into the trap of waffling on for too long in the first paragraph. The temptation is to rely on superfluous biographical or historical material rather than engaging with the terms of the question in a direct way that establishes the essay and the problem being discussed. In other words, use the beginning positively. Look at this opening paragraph of an essay on the novelist William Thackeray. The question title was 'Thackeray will always be seen as less radical than Dickens':

Thackeray was at one time seen as the equal of, even superior to, his contemporary Charles Dickens. Even in his lifetime, however, there were reservations, a sense that Thackeray was old-fashioned. Yet it is possibly the 'old-fashioned' qualities of Thackeray that make him interesting, for his is an awkward voice resisting the new assumptions at the heart of much mid-Victorian writing.

Can you see how the issue is set up, but does not outstay its welcome? The paragraph anticipates, but it does no more than raise expectations. We are prepared for an essay that will in the first section give us a sense of the nature of Thackeray's works, then go on in the next section to explain the ways in which they might be considered old-fashioned, before finally, in the third section, trying to define the unusual power that the writer of the essay sees as resulting from Thackeray's old-fashioned approach.

It is easy to underestimate this kind of opening. Some people prefer to start with a résumé of the essay, saying exactly what the argument is going to be and spelling out the conclusions. That is fine: it tells the reader what to expect and what to look out for, as in a report or technical document. The opening above also tells the reader what to expect and what conclusions might emerge by outlining the three topics that will form the substance of the essay and the problem being discussed. But it also manages to suggest that the final conclusions the essay will draw may be more complicated than we might expect and not lend themselves to simple summary. The opening, that is, leaves room for the essay to develop and also to arrive somewhere rather than being all over in the first paragraph.

Arriving somewhere

That leads us on to our final point about putting an essay together. A lot of students' essays drift off course towards the end. The student starts confidently, but the essay then fails to arrive anywhere. It helps if you think in terms of the structure we have been emphasising: setting the issue up, pushing it along and seeing where you arrive. But there is a slight modification that can enable you to insert more interest in the last stage of an essay. The formula we recommend to our students is, 'Set it up, push it along, then push your luck.' In other words, if you have worked solidly for two-thirds of the essay, your essay will make more of an impression if, in the last third, you push the essay into a new or slightly risky area.

Let us consider that you had been asked to write about the benefits of a certain food in people's diet. You might start with the facts and received knowledge about this food; the middle third of the essay might outline the benefits as established in the solid research of recent years; in the last third, however, you could take a risk by reporting on some aspects of the cutting-edge research on the subject. In other words, say sensible, and safe, things for two-thirds of the essay, then take a risk. In our Thackeray example above, the essay outlined a 'safe' view, before pushing its luck in the last third with a more contentious view of Thackeray's special quality.

To take another example: a general essay on the feminist movement in the twentieth century might start with the first seventy years of the century, then go on in the middle section to the period 1970–90, but then you might, in the final section, want to introduce complications relating to the present. An essay on Britain's place in Europe might start with the context and general picture (the recent history of Britain's relationship with Europe), then move on to the present state of affairs, but then become more speculative in the last third as it considers Britain's future role in Europe.

The general message of what we are saying is that a good essay is simple in structure but complex in content. Poor essay writers always tie themselves up in knots. A confident essay writer should be able to divide any topic into three sections. Each section of the essay should represent a clear stage in the argument, and each paragraph should represent a clear step forward in the argument.

There is, though, one final point we want to make in this section. It is often suggested that students who get first-class marks or first-class degrees challenge the question from the outset, that instead of building an answer they start with the risky material and take off from there. This may be the case, but they are also usually students who have got their essay method and writing worked out in fine detail. There is nothing off the cuff about what they do; rather, it is very often a carefully judged performance, with the student knowing exactly what they are doing and why. Our advice does not differ from this: if you know how to structure your essay, the chances are that you will know how to make the best of your ideas.

▶ Constructing a paragraph

The three-step formula that we have described for establishing overall control of an essay represents a logical form of organisation that can also be applied to the construction of a paragraph. Far too many students have very little idea quite where they are heading in any paragraph of an essay, but the fact is that every paragraph can and should be tightly, and even self-consciously, organised. Just as an essay as a whole sets up an issue, advances and arrives somewhere, so each paragraph of an essay needs to locate itself, advance and arrive somewhere new.

If you look back at the opening paragraph of the Thackeray essay in the last section you should be able to see that it conforms to this pattern. It actually consists of three sentences which fulfil these three functions. In a rather similar way, this opening paragraph of an essay on Mary Kinglsey, a Victorian traveller and writer, and the problem of 'place' starts with a 'topic' sentence that locates the issue, then advances by elaborating on that, finally arriving somewhere new. We have marked (/) the three steps of the paragraph:

> The life and works of Mary Kingsley illustrate the different relationship men and women often experience towards 'place'. / For men, the image of home is likely to suggest security, confidence, and nourishment. For women, however, home can prove to be just the opposite: a place of oppression, work, and perhaps even physical and sexual abuse. / In order to escape this oppressive sense of home, Kingsley detached herself from it by travelling 'away' to Africa, where she would experience a new sense of place.

Very efficiently, the issue has been located, the paragraph has advanced, and in no time at all has arrived somewhere new. In the essay as a whole, the student (in section one) elaborated on the sense of oppression Kingsley felt at home, then (in section two) considered the sense of liberation she experienced in Africa, but then (in the third, rather more risky, section of the essay) moved on to a complication, that Kingsley in Africa became an oppressor, just as other people had oppressed her at home. So, while the introduction set the essay up, the student then took advantage of that clear start to see how far she could take things. Section one was about oppression, section two about Africa, but then in section three the complications in the topic were brought out further than the opening paragraph initially suggests. That is because the student was using the essay structure to full advantage: while the first two stages deal with the complications of the topic, the final stage takes the essay on, breaking new ground with new ideas about the way in which Kingsley re-created the oppressive tyranny of home in Africa.

This three-part structure works well in the opening paragraph of an essay, and is just as effective in the body of an essay. This is the third paragraph of a student's essay looking at the poetry of T. S. Eliot from the viewpoint of feminist literary criticism:

> Feminist criticism is concerned with locating the place of women in an oppressive patriarchy. In Eliot's 'The Love Song of Alfred J. Prufrock' the

references are masculine: Michelangelo and Shakespeare, Lazarus and John the Baptist. Throughout history, men are deified, whereas women remain anonymous. / Yet Eliot's poem is a love poem, presumably addressed to a woman. Her questioning of the man, however, is subdued, and when a female voice is introduced it is only conveyed through Prufrock's narrative. Women are, in fact, mainly represented in abstract terms, through images such as arms, bracelets and shawls, and at times as a perfumed figure of temptation. / The associations are stereotypical. Prufrock's disjointed reflections avoid the whole woman, as if in fear. The woman is incomplete in poetry, just as she is unequal and incomplete in society.

This is quite complex work, but it is also very organised. The student locates the topic by identifying the masculine atmosphere of the poem; he or she then advances by considering how this is revealed in the poem; and then finally arrives at a running conclusion for the essay, which here takes the form of a fairly ambitious claim about how women are seen both in poetry and life. At this stage, the end of the first section of the essay (paragraph three in an eight-paragraph scheme of things), the student is ready to move on and push the argument along in the second section.

The method, then, is essentially a 'rule of three': start the paragraph with one or more topic sentences that locate where the argument has arrived at by this stage of the essay; in the body of the paragraph, look at the evidence. The movement from the opening to the middle of the paragraph is a movement from a general sentence to more precise and particular sentences. Then, having considered the evidence, as a third move, try to stand back a little at the end of a paragraph. One of the advantages of a paragraph constructed along these lines is that it serves the needs of your reader. At the start of each paragraph, you lead the reader into the issue. You then confront the reader with the evidence. Then, at the end of each paragraph, you pull the threads together for the reader. By stepping back a little in this kind of way at the end of each paragraph, you are also asserting your control over the overall movement and development of the essay.

▶ Constructing a sentence

Writing an essay is supposed to be both enjoyable and rewarding. The experience of a lot of people, however, is that the words just will not come, and if the words do come they won't do what they want them to do. Because essay writing can be difficult, it helps if you rely on methods such as our rule of three to help you get organised, and to move along. The great advantage is that you are not starting from a position of being totally lost. The rule of three gives you a kind of map of how to get through the essay as a whole, and it also gives you a kind of map of how to get through each paragraph. Some students say to us that such a method would impose excessive limits on their freedom and ability to express their ideas in an essay; and doubtless some teachers will be appalled at the idea of students knowing in advance how many paragraphs they are going to write and what the shape of the essay will be. Many students, however, appreciate how liberating such a disciplined method is; as so much of the effort of organising an essay is taken care of in advance, they can really concentrate on making the content of each paragraph and each sentence as strong as possible.

What we are recommending is essentially a template, and a template that encourages originality in the content of an essay rather than in the organisation of paragraphs. It might also be useful to know that the three-step logic that we have been describing in relation to essays as a whole and paragraphs can also be applied to individual sentences. We have described, in chapters 1 and 4, the rules about constructing a sentence, but it might help (particularly if you get stuck in trying to formulate a sentence) to think of sentences in terms of three parts: you start with the simple idea that you want to set up; then (if you move beyond the most simple sentence) you introduce any complications and elaborations, remembering to control the sentence very firmly; and then, finally, you need to check that the sentence has arrived somewhere. Each sentence, then, does on a smaller scale what each paragraph and the essay as whole does. If you are aware of that, you are likely to see how your sentences work to advance and contribute to the overall argument.

We want to look at just one sentence, chosen at random, to illustrate this way of thinking about analysing a sentence. Joseph Conrad's short novel *Heart of Darkness* begins:

> The *Nellie*, a cruising yawl, swung to her anchor without a flutter of the sails, and was at rest.

The most simple sentence within this is **The 'Nellie' swung to her anchor**. We could analyse the sentence in the terms we employed in chapters 1 and 4, thinking about the phrases that have been added, and the use of the compound sentence structure. But we can also think in three steps: the topic is the ship, the *Nellie*, at anchor. But in order to advance this simple proposition, additional information is introduced into the sentence. Conrad does this through inserting the phrase *a cruising yawl* and the adverbial phrase *without a flutter of the sails*. These extra details open the sentence up, but it also has to close down again, and anyone writing a crafted sentence such as this has to take stock as the full stop is written. Has the sentence arrived somewhere? Does it hold together? This essentially means, does it make sense (which it will only do if it follows the rules about sentence construction and punctuation)?

► **Summary**

The whole time, in putting an essay together, you are setting something up, advancing and then taking stock of where you arrive. This is true of each sentence, each paragraph and the essay as a whole. Of course, when you are writing an essay you might have no wish, or find it quite unnecessary, to check on this mechanical orderliness of each stage of your work. But at all those points where you get stuck in writing (and everyone does get stuck), it is helpful to say to yourself: 'Can I move through three steps in order to solve the problem I have got myself into here?' Our experience, and the experience of many of our students, is that such an approach really does help

8 Punctuation and Presentation

Success in writing depends upon attention to the overall structure of your work, the topic of the previous chapter, and also attention to detail. That includes making sure that sentences are grammatical and correctly punctuated and spelt, as well as a host of little presentational details that you should strive to get right. Punctuation is one vital aspect of how your work is presented to your reader, but there is something closely related to punctuation, most commonly referred to as the mechanics of presentation. These are conventions rather than absolute rules about writing, but it helps the reader of an essay if your work is presented in accordance with the conventions of an established code.

What we are referring to includes such things as the presentation of direct speech, but it also takes in the physical appearance of your work on the page, the mechanics for handling quotations, and little things such as the use of ellipses (we'll explain later) and why foreign words and phrases have to be underlined or put in italics. We don't attempt to explain every aspect of presentation in this chapter since quite a lot of it is of interest only to editors and publishers. However, we do try to deal with most of the questions about presentation that are likely to crop up during the course of writing an essay and which will help you communicate your ideas and argument in a clear way.

▶ Direct speech

We have referred a number of times to the fact that there is a world of difference between speaking and writing. Often, in conversation, people tell stories or anecdotes to their friends; they can always signal very clearly what people said, and what was said in return. This is an amazingly sophisticated verbal performance that just about everybody in society can handle with great confidence: they mimic other people's voices, or in some way suggest their speech patterns, or preface other speaker's words with the sound 'Oo', conveying the sense of another voice. It is impossible to match such effects in writing. We do, none the less, need a conventional system to convey speech. There is, fortunately, a well-established, and straightforward, set of conventions for this.

We will start with the most simple case. If someone is speaking, and you are reporting directly the words actually used, you need double inverted commas to signal their words, plus full stops and commas in specific places:

"Push off," said the night-club bouncer.

As you can see, there are double inverted commas at the start of what he says and at the conclusion of what he says. There is a comma after *off*, and inside the inverted commas (or speech marks). That is because the sentence continues. If the sentence did not continue, there would be a full stop inside the speech marks:

"Push off." The night-club bouncer glared at me.

If this was reported speech, rather than direct speech, the speech marks would not be required: *The nightclub bouncer told me to push off, and went on to add that he was under the impression I was looking for a poke in the eye*. If the sentence of direct speech is interrupted, the sentence would appear as follows:

"Push off. Are you looking," he snarled, "for a poke in the eye? I hate students."

As the sentence of direct speech has been interrupted, the second unit starts with a lower-case letter.

A lot of times, however, a new sentence will start after the words *he said* or *he snarled*. And, as it is a new sentence, it will start with a capital letter:

"Well, you are rather above yourself for such a lowly minion," I replied. "Would you care to provide me with your name in order that I can report you to the chairman of the multinational company that operates this leisure venue?"

If the other speaker replies, this means the start of another paragraph:

> . . . operates this leisure venue?"
> "Now look here," he said, "there's a limit to my patience, but I'll make the assumption that you are only joking." And with that he threw me out.

Single or double inverted commas?

Most people are, in fact, aware of the conventions governing the presentation of direct speech, though they may not always remember to employ them when required. There are, however, some details about the application of the rules we can feel unsure about. One is whether single or double speech marks should be used for direct speech; the cause of the uncertainty here is that many publishers of fiction, such as Penguin, nowadays prefer single speech marks. There is, in fact, no right or wrong about this; it is an arbitrary convention, and the choice is up to you. Generally, however, in creative work writers stick to double for dialogue and, as we will see in the next section, single in academic work when quoting from a book, article, magazine, etc. The trend is likely to move towards employing single all the time, to avoid having to switch from one to another, but it is perfectly acceptable to stick to double for speech and single elsewhere as long as you are consistent. Another little convention to be aware of is that if one person speaks for several paragraphs in your written version of their words, you reuse speech marks at the start of each paragraph, but only use them to conclude at the end of the final paragraph that originated from that one speaker.

There is sometimes uncertainty about where a closing question mark is positioned. The answer, however, is logical. If the question is in the direct speech, the question mark is inside the speech marks:

> I asked the nurse, "Where am I?"

But sometimes the whole sentence, rather than the unit enclosed, is the question, and in these circumstances the question mark must go outside the speech marks:

> What possessed me to say to that bouncer, "Hello sailor"?

Another occasion when a punctuation mark appears outside the speech marks is if you use a semicolon in the sentence:

> I continued, "Come on, if you think you're hard"; yet even as I spoke, I feared the worst.

And that more or less covers direct speech conventions. It might, of course, be the case that you do not need to use these at all at university, as they are conventions that are more common in creative writing than academic writing. You might notice, however, that some writers – James Joyce is the leading example – ignore the convention; he dismisses speech marks as 'perverted commas'.

▶ Presentation conventions

We now want to move on to the various conventions that relate to the presentation of written work, particularly the kind of work produced by university students. For this we have identified a 'Fifteen to Follow' list. Several of these points are bound to come up in any essay you write; it is, therefore, well worth checking through the list to see if you are presenting your work in an appropriate way. It is just this kind of attention to detail that surreptitiously picks up more marks for you in an essay, but also helps you to develop a polished and professional approach to written work.

1. Spacing work

A word-processed essay should always be double-spaced (set your word-processor to print on every other line). Generous spacing makes your essay easier to read, and leaves room for the marker to write in comments. The main secret of typing essays is always to allow plenty of space on the page: sensible margins (at least 25 mm), double spacing, a reasonably large font or typeface (we suggest not smaller thant 11 point text). Think of the needs of your reader; your reader wants to be presented with something that is easy on the eye, and as such easy to read.

Your aim in word-processing (or, more rarely these days, typing) an essay is to present an impression of your competence, and the look of your work is part and parcel of this overall impression. Remember that mistakes in spelling and punctuation may be far more apparent, and glaring, in a printed essay than they are in a hand-written essay. You should also remember, therefore, that it is your responsibility to proof-read and spell-check your essay for errors. Don't make the mistake of thinking just because you have spent a lot of time on your choice of fonts that the marker will ignore your errors. The very opposite: he or she will see that you have put trivial things before important matters. So, the lesson is well-presented work is a must – and that includes reading it through for mistakes. A useful tip is to leave the work for a while after it is finished and then to check the print-out (it's virtually impossible to check work as a whole on the screen). This, of course, implies that you haven't left everything until the last minute. Markers can always spot a script that has been dashed off just before the deadline: invariably, it will have mistakes in the opening paragraph, and sometimes in the title, too.

2. Titles

At school most people are taught to put all titles in single inverted commas (e.g. **'Hamlet'**). At university and more generally in publishing, however, the accepted convention is that book titles are underlined or put in italics (e.g. <u>Hamlet</u> or *Hamlet*). Single inverted commas, by contrast, indicate names of poems, or short stories, or chapter titles that appear in other books. We would, therefore, write **'Ode to a Nightingale'** for a poem, but *The Waste Land* if the poem has been published on its own, as a book under such a title. The rule, therefore, is that titles are underlined, but you put single inverted commas, or quotation marks, around the titles of works that are a part of other works. We should add that underlining in an essay represents italics. These days most students can word-process their essays and many opt for italics instead of underlining. But in exams, of course, it is not possible to do this, and underlining becomes the only method available. In general, it is probably best to keep to underlining both in essays and examinations so that you have a consistent system to employ. In preparing this book, for example, everything that is now in italics was originally underlined; this told the printer where to employ italic. It is possibly worth explaining that many of the conventions used in academic work relate to the needs of publishers to ensure the standard presentation of their books. Almost every publisher has its own 'house style' for layout. In a sense, what we are recommending is a version of the standard academic house style, where you use the signals and signs that belong to formal writing.

3. Foreign words and phrases

Foreign words and phrases that have not been fully absorbed into English should be underlined or put in italics, although some people put them in inverted commas. A phrase such as 'status quo' is so widely used in English that it need not be underlined or italicised, but words and phrases that are not so well established should be: 'Short hair is currently *de rigueur* for English footballers.' Oddly, the names of ships should also be underlined or italicised (e.g. *HMS Fearless)*.

4. Setting out quotations: prose

The obvious point to make about quotations is that they act as evidence for the case or argument you are making in an essay. Like evidence in a court of law, they need to be given accurately. The golden rule with quotations is to set the material out exactly as it appears in your source.

If you quote a few words (and remember the noun is quotation: 'quote' is too colloquial for formal work), you run the words on in the text of your essay on the same line. Logic suggests whether a colon, a comma or no punctuation mark at all precedes the quotation:

> Dickens opens his novel with the words 'Thirty years ago, Marseilles lay burning in the sun, one day'.

> We can see this in the opening words of the novel: 'Thirty years ago, Marseilles lay burning . . . one day.'

> As the narrator reminds us at the start of Dickens's novel, 'Thirty years ago, Marseilles lay burning in the sun, one day.'

That is how we set up a quotation. The only real difference between them is that in the first example there is no punctuation before the quotation, and so the full stop is placed outside the closing inverted comma. In the second example, we have inserted three dots (known as an ellipsis) to show we have cut the sentence. You can use the ellipsis if you miss out words at the beginning or at the end of a sentence, but that is not really necessary. You would, however, use an ellipsis if you cut out words between two sentences.

These very minor details can sometimes get in the way of presenting an essay simply and logically. The great rule is to be consistent. Our own practice is to place a full stop inside the closing inverted comma provided the quotation is preceded by a punctuation mark and forms a complete sentence:

> In the words of Evelyn Waugh, 'Quotation is a national vice.'

Longer quotations

If you wish to include a longer quotation (three or more typed lines), you should indent it. You do not put inverted commas around such a quotation; the fact that you have indented it signals that it is a quotation. Such quotations should be single-spaced rather than double-spaced. You do not use a paragraph indentation at the start of the quotation even if it is the start of a paragraph. But you would for the second paragraph if your quotation was so long that it went on to include a second paragraph. In the following example, the first sentence of the essay sets up the indented quotation:

> Martin Luther King's words still retain their power:

> > I have a dream that one day on the red hills of Georgia the sons of former slaves and the sons of former slave owners will be able to sit down together at the table of brotherhood.

Longer quotations are in some ways easier to handle than short ones, but a judicious mix in an essay will be more interesting to your reader. A skill in writing is weaving in shorter quotations into your own prose, but also selecting appropriate longer quotations for analysis. The key point to remember with longer extracts is that you do not need inverted commas if you indent a quotation. If the quotation includes direct speech, however, then you would keep the speech marks since they are actually part of the quoted material.

5. Setting out quotations: poetry

The rules for quoting poetry are, in essence, exactly the same as for prose quotations. If you are quoting just a single line from a poem (or from a song or a verse play), you run the line on into your own text. The same points about punctuation apply as for prose:

> Yeats opens his poem with the line 'Turning and turning in the widening gyre / The falcon cannot hear the falconer'.

> The opening of Yeats's poem is: 'Turning and turning in the widening gyre / The falcon cannot hear the falconer.'

> As Yeats says at the beginning of his poem, 'Turning and turning in the widening gyre / The falcon cannot hear the falconer.'

It is the rule that you produce the quotation as it is in your text. Accuracy is important: checking immediately and a second time later can help. The best advice is to present the text exactly as it appears even if this means a capital letter appearing in the middle of a sentence: *Marvell writes of 'My vegetable love'*. This is perfectly clear and understandable. Even if we do not understand the Marvell words, we can guess that *My* starts a new line in his poem. Poetry quotations of one or two lines may be incorporated into your text. If you do quote two lines, mark the end of the first line by a slash: **'Hi, ho, hi, ho / It's off to work we go.'**

If you wish to include a quotation of more than two lines, you should indent them. As with prose, you do not use quotation marks because the indentation takes their place:

> Christina Rossetti's best lines are always powerful in their evocation of death and love:

> Remember me when I am gone away,
>   Gone far away into the silent land;
>   When you can no more hold me by the hand,
> Nor I half turn to go yet turning stay.

Because poetry depends in part on being recognised as poetry to work, it is important, as here, to maintain the presentation details of the text.

6. Setting out quotations: drama

Not surprisingly, the rules about quotations from plays are basically the same as for prose and poetry. There are slight variations because we are dealing with a different genre, but the overall codes and conventions are the same. Indeed, presentation of quotations is one area where you really can achieve consistency quite easily. As we noted above, you will discover that different publishers employ different formats, and there are differences between American and British academic writing, but following just one set of guidelines is obviously the most sensible course. So, for short quotations from drama we employ exactly the same layout as for prose:

> Lady Macbeth's first words to Macbeth are 'Great Glamis! Worthy Cawdor!'

> Lady Macbeth begins her address to Macbeth thus: 'Great Glamis! Worthy Cawdor!'

> As Lady Macbeth notes, 'Great Glamis! Worthy Cawdor!' are now Macbeth's titles.

If the quotation is longer than two lines, you may well find it necessary to give the names of the characters speaking as well as to indent the extract:

> SERGEANT: Halt! Who are you with, you trash?
> THE ELDER SON: Second Finnish Regiment.
> SERGEANT: Where's your papers?
> MOTHER COURAGE: Papers?

In all of these cases the logic is the same. The short quotation is worked into the texture of your essay (with appropriate punctuation), while the longer extract is set off in an indentation to draw attention to it as a significant part of your evidence.

There are two minor notes to add to this information. We usually introduce indented quotations by a colon at the end of the sentence before, as we have just illustrated above with the quotation from Brecht's play *Mother Courage*. Sometimes, however, it may be that the quotation forms part of the sentence that introduces the quotation. For example, we might be discussing Lady Macbeth's greeting of Macbeth with his new titles and how, as she says,

> Thy letters have transported me beyond
> This ignorant present, and I feel now
> The future in the instant.

Here the quotation fits in grammatically with the sentence we have devised, so a colon is not required. The effect of a colon before a quotation is to make a break between the sentence and the quotation that follows, as if you were saying, 'Here is the evidence; look at this.'

The second point to make about indented quotations is that it is much better to avoid wrapping sentences around them. In other words, it is best not to have a sentence that introduces an indented quotation and then continues after the quotation. The reader is unlikely to remember the part of the sentence before the quotation and so will have to go back to try and work out the point you are making. The result will be that the relevance of the quotation will get lost. Wrap-around sentences rarely work: they are invariably too long, and their syntax (the grammatical relations between words) is usually very shaky. Stylistically they look awkward and they raise all sorts of knotty problems about punctuation – do you end the quotation with a dash, or a comma, or a full stop or nothing at all? The simple answer is to avoid the problem in the first place.

7. Quotations within quotations

In the words of Winston Churchill, 'The maxim of the British people is "Business as Usual".' If there is a second quotation within the first quotation, it is signalled by double inverted commas, to indicate its distinct identity as a separate unit within the quotation. (You might wonder why we have used single quotation marks here rather than double for speech, but here we are not dealing with dialogue as such.) A variant of this is titles within titles. If we have a book called *Dickens's Vision in 'Bleak House'*, the entire title of the book is underlined or in italics, but we also need inverted commas, on this occasion, around *Bleak House* to signal that it is a book title within the other book title.

This might be a convenient point to add another function for inverted commas, which is to highlight a word, or set it up as a special term for the first time. For example, in this book, when we first referred to a 'simple' sentence we put it in inverted commas to signal that this was a word being used in a precise way. Indeed, this is exactly what many books do in discussing terms and terminology as well as foreign words in order to highlight them. In the end we opted for bold to make the technical terms stand out, but in an essay you would use inverted commas. One practice to be cautious about, however, is the use of 'scare quotes' or 'sneer quotes', that is, using quotation marks as if the word you are discussing should not be understood in its usual sense. For example, academics often put the word 'natural' in quotation marks so as to question whether something really is natural; or they might write about the 'meaning' of a text. The effect can be to leave the reader uncertain quite what it is that is being questioned or quoted; or, if overused, the result can turn the essay into a riot of quotation marks.

8. Altering quotations

There may be times when you need to add or alter words in a quotation, so that it will make sense in the context of your essay. For example, here we have added a character's name to help the quotation make sense: *Malcolm Muggeridge said that '[Macmillan] exuded a flavour of mothballs'*. Square brackets are used around the interpolated matter. You might also need to alter a quotation if you are using a quotation with a lower case letter at the outset, but want to use it to start a sentence:

> '[T]he lady's not for turning' is just one example of Margaret Thatcher's striking use of literary allusions for political ends.

Square brackets show that material has been added or altered. As we have noted above, ellipsis marks (three stops) have the opposite function, indicating an omission from a quotation:

> A man . . . is so in the way in the house. (Elizabeth Gaskell)

There is a space, then the three stops, then a space. If a sentence had been concluded after *A man*, there would have been a stop, without a space, then three stops, as in this example:

> Photography can never grow up if it imitates some other medium. . . . it has to be itself.

If you want to omit a line or several lines from a poem you are quoting, you put an ellipsis at the end of the previous line before the omission, as in this example from Donne:

> Busy old foole, unruly sunne . . .
> She is all States, all Princes I

As with all such devices, the best advice is not to overuse them, but they are worth knowing about because they are used in academic writing and it is as well to understand the conventions you are working with. It is the case, though, that you could write hundreds of essays and never encounter a single occasion on which you needed to edit a quotation in the ways described. They are usually changes made necessary by the context in which they are placed. Really, it is another case where, as with so much in presentation, a little bit of common sense together with consistent usage will see you through.

9. Parentheses

We refer to these just as commonly as brackets (which is what the square ones [ ] are called). We use them to contain parenthetical expressions. If you use brackets, rather than commas, it indicates that this is a kind of digression in the sentence. We might often include dates in this way: *Charles Dickens (1812–70)*. Don't put a comma before the brackets; if a comma or full stop is used after the brackets, it should be positioned outside the closing parentheses. However, you may add a complete sentence in parentheses, in which case the stops would appear within the brackets:

> The comma after parentheses (or brackets) is not always necessary. (But there are times when a stop is included inside, as in this example.)

10. The dash

'This sort of thing may be tolerated by the French, but we are British – thank God' (Montgomery of Alamein). The dash should be used very sparingly. As in this example, it should be used to create a particular effect, and sometimes in sentences when material is inserted – we can't think of an example – but very rarely. It is intended as a strong punctuation mark, that is, to indicate a violent break in the flow of the sentence. Notice that, like brackets and parentheses (which are weak interruptions to a sentence), dashes come in pairs – unless at the end of a sentence. We would issue a warning against the dash. It disrupts and interrupts – especially if used several times in a paragraph. It is most common in dialogue in plays and novels where it is much more appropriate. Finally, do not confuse the dash with the hyphen: hyphens join words; dashes separate them.

11. The slash

The circumstances in which you might require a slash are very few. The slash is used to separate lines of poetry that are run on in the text, and between options. Note the spacing: 'Has anybody here seen Kelly? / Kelly from the Isle of Man?' 'It was simply a pass/fail exam.' If it is an option (*hot/cold*) note the absence of spaces between the word and the slash and the next word. In terms of style it is better to write 'hot or cold'.

12. Abbreviations

Is it the BBC or the B.B.C? Is it Mr. Jones or Mr Jones. Is it a Ph.D. or a PhD? There is an increasing tendency to omit the stop in such abbreviations, but there are cases where many people still include it. For example, after *etc.*:

Smith, Jones, Brown, White, etc. must all report after school.

And some others: *e.g.*, *i.e.*, though here again usage is moving more and more towards *eg* and *ie*. In formal writing, however, these abbreviations are best avoided.

13. Number

If you insert a number in the text, when do you use the word (ten) and when do you use the number? A common convention is to use words to ten and then numbers thereafter.

14. Capital letters

We dealt with this topic in chapter 3 where we pointed out the tendency towards the use of fewer capital letters. For example, we would now write 'prime minister', but keep 'President of the United States'. There is a sense in which this marks a slight change in the conventions, but the basic rules have not changed. Capital letters are still used for most words in the titles of books (although librarians use only the initial capital letter), for a specific person and for places, for historical events, political and social organisations, nationalities, proper names and religions. Occasionally you will come across someone who insists on defying such conventions by, for example, writing 'english' with a lower case 'e', but this kind of playing with the conventions is best not imitated in an essay.

15. References

Whenever you quote, or use material from a source, you need to provide a reference, showing the source of your quotation or information. This would either appear in parentheses at the end of the quotation or relevant sentence, or would be footnoted, or as an endnote, a number in superscript signalling the note. We thought long and hard about whether to include advice on references, but decided against it, as the conventions vary from subject to subject. You will probably have been provided with a style sheet for references as part of your course and you will need to follow whatever recommendations are given in it.

▶ Summary

This might seem an exceptionally fussy and pedantic chapter. Is it really necessary to get all these little things right? All we can say is that the people who get a good degree result usually have bothered to acquire a confident knowledge of all these small conventions of presentation. This is because in the end, as we noted in the introduction to the chapter, the conventions are just part and parcel of a generally professional approach to academic work: you signal to the reader the quality of your thinking by the quality of your presentation. Conversely, if you neglect all aspects of presentation, it is likely that you will lose marks. There are lots of little rules here, but essentially it is a matter of common sense: you present your work in a way that communicates its meaning most effectively to your readers, that is, in a clear unambiguous way. This really leads us on to the subject matter of our final chapter: writing is not a private activity; it is (with obvious exceptions such as diaries, lecture notes and so on) always for an audience. And that means always finding the right tone, the right level and the right words for your readership.

9 The Right Word

Writing, as we have said, is a matter of arriving at the right words in the right order. If you can achieve that, at some stage you have crossed the line from writing merely competently to writing with style. For many people, particularly when producing an academic essay, language is merely a kind of wheelbarrow for trundling their ideas around. There comes a point, however, when the reader begins to notice just how well written some essays are (possibly they notice in a negative way, in the sense that they suddenly realise an essay has been effortless to read, that the writer has swept them through the topic with poise and assurance). A great deal of what is involved in writing with style is a matter of following the rules and paying attention to detail; the last two chapters, in particular, have dealt with how to achieve a professional level of structural organisation and polished presentation in your work, and these are important aspects of writing with style. But perhaps the real key lies in the skill with which good writers invariably find the right word and forge the right phrase. It is only with practice that one can achieve such assurance in writing, but in this chapter we try to suggest some of the things to be aware of in making the move from competence to writing with style. We might sum these up as being self-conscious about your grammar, word order and vocabulary, and then taking great care that your work is clear and correct. All of these things will give your work readability and authority. Don't be fooled by the word 'style', however; it doesn't involve long, elaborate sentences and esoteric vocabulary. The basis of all good writing is the simple, well-constructed sentence serving the needs both of your reader and of your ideas.

▶ **Addressing the reader**

Style starts with being aware of your reader. This is why we have stressed the importance of presenting your ideas in an orderly way in an essay, and that you should always be striving for correctness. You should never be prepared to tolerate sloppiness or laziness in the composition of your work. Every essay you write is the equivalent of a job interview. It is a performance where you have to put on your best clothes, if only for the day, and behave in a way that is designed to impress. You want to be seen at your best. Just as turning up in your most comfortable old clothes for a job interview would be inappropriate behaviour, a certain fussiness over making sure that sentences are well constructed and well presented is essential in an essay. In this way you will ensure that your writing fits in with the pattern of standard English, the norm in education, business and the professions. Your reader expects to be able to understand what you write, and also expects that you will be trying to communicate efficiently. None of these points, however, should be worrying, for, as we have stressed throughout, there are a very small number of rules about writing that you need to follow; if you know how to construct and punctuate a sentence, you can be sure that you won't go far wrong.

There are, though, other aspects to writing that it is useful to be aware of. Consider this sentence:

> The reader who immerses himself in Wordsworth's poem feels that he has gained a sense of the importance of the poet's relationship with nature.

This, of course, raises the question of gender in writing: the author has identified the reader as a 'he', so excluding half the population. The reasons for avoiding sexist thinking of this kind have to do with recognising that language is a very powerful instrument for shaping the world we live in. The effect of using 'he' not only makes women invisible, but also, implicitly, suggests women are less important than men. Often this may be a matter of unconscious bias: a student, for example, writing an essay about the education system might use exclusively male examples, or a student writing a politics essay might write as if the central roles are the natural preserve of men. It is important to recognise that such bias, even if it is an unconscious bias, is no longer acceptable in academic work. There is, too, another side to this. At university you are meant to be looking at things from new angles, considering things in ways that you might not have done before. If you use sexist terms you are, essentially, clinging to a traditional world-view; if you consciously avoid sexist language, this is a way in which you can make yourself aware of how you are trying to shift your ground, how you are identifying with the need to look at things in a way that breaks with old habits of perception.

That, however, is vague and general advice. What is it, more precisely, that you need to be alert to in writing an essay? First, never use the term 'he' on its own in the way it was used in the sentence above about Wordsworth. An alternative is to use 'he or she', or 'she or he', or even 's/he', but a more sensible answer is to construct a sentence where the personal pronoun is not required:

> The result of immersing oneself in Wordsworth's poem is a feeling of gaining a sense of the importance of the poet's relationship with nature.

That is one way of replacing it, although it would be even better to cut out much of the waffle in the sentence:

> Wordworth's poem offers a sense of the importance of his relationship with nature.

Here is another good reason for avoiding sexist language, forced to rephrase a sentence, you might well be surprised at the kind of brevity you can achieve, a brevity in which not a word is wasted and where the main point comes through more clearly.

The issue of address, however, extends well beyond the avoidance of 'he'. You should aim to avoid any discriminatory language, that is, language showing bias against any group. This isn't a matter of 'political correctness'; it's a matter of thinking who your reader might be. This is, again, a case of stepping outside inherited patterns of thinking. Do not, for example, make the assumption in your writing that doctors and airline pilots are male, while nurses and cabin staff are female. Avoid stereotyped terms for describing people: for instance, the idea that males in positions of authority show qualities of leadership, whereas women are bossy. Rationality is not a virtue that is peculiarly associated with men, and women do not possess special qualities of intuition. If you think about it for a moment, can you see how in many subjects rejection of these old assumptions will enable you to consider issues in a fresh and original way? Obviously one should avoid terms such as chairman (use chairperson or chair), policeman (police officer) and lady (woman). In a business letter, use the person's name if possible. If you do not know it, and are unsure of the gender of the person you are addressing, use 'Dear Sir or Madam'. The salutation 'Dear Sir' maintains a redundant perception that the sphere of business is the exclusive preserve of men.

As we have noted above, the problem of how to avoid 'he' and 'him' is often solved simply by changing the structure. For example, by switching to a plural pronoun:

Each student must complete his assignments before the vacation.

It would be much better to reconstruct this sentence as follows:

All students must complete their assignments before the vacation.

Or the sentence can be changed to the passive:

All student assignments must be completed before the vacation.

We hope that what we have said sounds totally reasonable. What we have tried to explain here is simply a matter of good manners, of showing consideration, of not gratuitously insulting or patronising any person or group. But as we have also attempted to show, making the effort in respect of something like this also has benefits for you as a student. It will help you think in different ways; this kind of attention to the detail of language will also make you alert to the resonance of words, to just how judiciously the words have to be selected in an essay, to how language carries values and overtones. This takes us on to our next topic, which is judging the appropriate tone in which to write.

▶ Tone and vocabulary

Can you see anything wrong with this paragraph?

The risk of damnation is made clear in Kyd's *The Spanish Tragedy* by the use of a ghost from hell, called Revenge, who acts as a chorus to the play. This provides a formal framework which contrasts with the violent actions of the characters. There's also something rather spooky about a ghost.

If you feel that the last sentence struck the wrong note, it is because the word 'spooky' is inappropriate. But why? Isn't it a perfectly good word? It probably is, but the problem is that it's an informal word, the kind of word that might be used in conversation, but which jars with the formal tone required in an essay. You might also feel that it is a rather lightweight word. Up until that point the writer has achieved a good level of analysis, but the final sentence unintentionally trivialises the subject. For a moment the writer takes his/her eye off the topic and makes a rather vague, colloquial point. It is important in writing an essay to strive for a fairly formal tone. Contractions such as **didn't**, **wasn't** and **can't** are best avoided, as they tend to make an essay seem too relaxed and chatty. (We are, of course, aware that we have used them throughout this book, specifically as a way of achieving a certain degree of informality.) It is easy to see whether you have slipped into using words like these, but you might at times be unsure whether a word is formal enough for an essay, or perhaps too colloquial. We imagine that you are unlikely to use phrases like **Carol Ann Duffy is a really cool poet**, but if in doubt about a word or phrase, search for an alternative. A thesaurus will provide you with several alternatives for most words; your dictionary should tell you whether a word is slang or colloquial or archaic or whether you have made it up. A thesaurus or dictionary should also help you find the appropriate word with the right connotations.

What we are all seeking to achieve is a sensible but not stuffy tone to our writing. In part, the rules of sentence construction, including the points we have made about adding subordinate clauses to a sentence, will help you achieve this. But a reasonably wide choice and range of ordinary vocabulary is also essential. Oddly enough, however, a lot of university students make the mistake of veering in the other direction, using a vocabulary that is too pretentious, perhaps trying to echo or imitate the tone of the authors of the textbooks in their subject. This is not always done deliberately. It is the case that, in studying a subject, some of the vocabulary is silently absorbed and that part of learning a subject is coming to terms with its specialist language. Sometimes, however, this specialist language can become a kind of rhetorical smokescreen, the student hiding behind big words rather than using these to any good effect. Such a student might be trying to impress, but the result could be the very opposite.

What we are suggesting is that you should write clearly, and as intelligently as you can, but there is no need to strain after an artificial degree of elevation or to pack your work with the latest jargon. To a large extent it is a matter of finding your own style, your own level. A large part of this is seeing just how simple a lot of good writing is. Initially you might feel unhappy with your style, but a little practice experimenting with some of the points we have made throughout this book will soon remedy that. Rapid progress with style can, in fact, be made quite easily. Often it is a matter of avoiding the pitfalls and then working on small details.

Here we can highlight two points. First, it is sensible to look out for clichés in your writing. A cliché is a trite expression, a phrase that has been used so much that it has become stale and lost any real effect. For example:

cool, calm and collected	ripe old age
face the music	sadder but wiser
hard as a rock	

The effect of phrases such as these is to deaden your writing and make it seem mechanical and uninteresting for the reader. We often turn to clichés because they are the first words that come into our head, or we have got stuck for a phrase for a moment. Writing, however, needs to be a more considered performance than this. One of the things to look out for, then, as you revise your work are dead areas of writing where you may be using a cliché. Occasionally clichés can help, precisely because they are familiar and can help clinch a point, but the ones listed above are very colloquial; they work wonderfully well in speech, but lack the sort of precision we usually want in writing.

The second point is both a tip and a summary of everything we have been saying in this section. It can sometimes seem difficult to pitch your writing at the right level and to work out if you are conveying your ideas clearly. A way of overcoming this is literally to have a reader in mind (for example, your mum or dad) and to focus on making sure that the person you have in mind can follow the threads of your argument. Your reader should be able to spot that you are hitting the right note and that you are not, for example, showing off or writing just for yourself. Very often essays get tangled in knots because students forget that they are communicating to an audience; they are not teasing out a few points or ideas but seeking to inform, persuade and interest their readers. The key to this, as we have said, is control over the basic mechanics of writing: knowing how to write a sentence, how to punctuate, and using the right words.

▶ Finding a style

Most people would agree that the essence of good style is to say what you want to say as clearly as you can in as few words as possible. It is not always easy, however, to find agreement about how to achieve this. The writer George Orwell drew up some guidance on the topic. His advice was as follows:

1. Never use a metaphor, simile or other figure of speech which you are used to seeing in print.
2. Never use a long word where a short one will do.

3. If it is possible to cut a word out, always cut it out.
4. Never use the passive where you can use the active.
5. Never use a foreign phrase, a scientific word or a jargon word if you can think of an everyday English equivalent.
6. Break any of these rules sooner than say anything outright barbarous.

Orwell also offered some advice about the kind of questions to ask yourself when writing: 'What am I trying to say? What words will express it? What image or idiom will make it clearer? Is this image fresh enough to have an effect?' To these he added two more questions: 'Could I put it more shortly? Have I said anything that is avoidably ugly?'

The advice here is worth thinking about, but also worth questioning, too. As we noted above, clichés can sometimes be useful because they are familiar and so can help to get a point across. Using the passive form for sentences can give them a different focus and also add variety to your writing. Thus we might want to write:

The jury believed every word.

Or:

Every word was believed by the jury.

The effect of turning the sentence round like this is to reposition the emphasis: in the first instance attention focuses on the jury as the subject and their actions; in the second, the stress falls on the fact that they believed every word.

Orwell's point about not using long words seems sensible for a non-specialist audience, but if you are writing for a knowledgeable audience polysyllabic terms can sometimes be the quickest way of conveying something briefly and also demonstrate that you are knowledgeable about your topic. As we suggested above, keeping in mind the two basic questions we need to ask about writing – 'Who is the audience?' and 'What is the purpose?' – will provide you with a way of thinking about style. It is, however, also fair to say that ideas about style change as language and culture change. Orwell's advice was once regarded as timeless, but nowadays some of it looks old-fashioned and is out of favour. Language experts no longer talk about sentences being 'ugly', but do notice 'awkward' sentences, that is, sentences which don't flow easily or which don't offer their information clearly to the reader.

If you write an awkward sentence, or one that doesn't make any sense to you, change it. Sometimes this is a matter of rephrasing the point, sometimes of splitting a long sentence into two. Very often, though, it will be a combination of several grammatical errors piling up in a sentence, and when you sort these out the problem will disappear. Just occasionally, though, you might find the reason the sentence has gone wrong is that it is superfluous. It has become a 'dumping ground' for your ideas and you may find, therefore, that you can cut it altogether. A useful rule of thumb in this situation is 'write less, say more'.

Some things in terms of elegance of expression are easy to achieve. You might, for example, have heard of split infinitives, and know that they should be avoided, but you might not know what a split infinitive actually is. The famous phrase from *Star Trek* – **To boldly go** – where an adverb appears between the word **to** and the actual verb **go**, explains it all. Traditionalists always avoid split infinitives and argue that to never split (that is a very clear split infinitive) an infinitive should always be the aim in an essay. Contemporary practice is much more relaxed about the topic and suggests that split infinitives are now acceptable and simply reflect modern culture. The choice is yours: you should know what a split infinitive is and that some people consider it clumsy and uneducated, but in some circumstances it seems almost unavoidable and useful to both reader and writer.

Easier to avoid are clashes of sounds ('The debate about bats is belittling'), or awkward phrases and phrasing:

> With reference to your letter, as referred to in your later letter, we are sorry we did not receive this.

> The theatre can be seen as a site of struggle, regarding the status and function of the audience.

> Students will get their marks after the exam results are published after the examiners' meetings in the afternoon.

With things like this it is really only a matter of reading your work out loud to yourself, seeing whether it can be expressed in any way that is more attractive or elegant. Most authors, for example, try to avoid repeating a word in too close proximity; sometimes you may have to add words to expand the sentence in order to make sense, or sometimes divide a long sentence into two. While there are no magic rules about any of this, good sense will help you see that readability and length are not the same thing; that the longer sentences become, the more likely it is that they will run out of control; and that sentences have to work together, not in isolation. In themselves, however, long sentences are not obscure or unreadable; what matters is how you handle the elements in them and the relations between sentences.

Types of sentence

So far much of the advice we have offered about style may seem negative; it has been more about what to avoid than what to do. There are two reasons for this. One is the very simple reason that success in writing is built around very simple principles: you think about what you want to say and who you are writing for. There is, in a sense, not a lot more to add to this statement: it is the case that success is as much a matter of not making errors as of getting things right. But second, although it seems improbable, the main thing to realise is just how straightforward a lot of stylish and effective writing is.

A classic example often cited at this point is the novelist Ernest Hemingway, with his use of simple and compound sentences, and few adjectives or adverbs. This is from *To Have and Have Not*:

> At a little before eleven I saw the two lights show on the point. I waited a little while and then I took her in slow. Bacurano is a cove where there used to be a big dock for loading sand. There is a little river that comes in when the rains open the bar across the mouth. The northers, in the winter, pile the sand up and close it. They used to go in with schooners and load guavas from the river and there used to be a town. But the hurricane took it and it is all gone now except one house some gallegos built out of the shacks the hurricane blew down and that they use for a clubhouse on Sundays when they come out to swim and picnic from Havana. There is one other house where the delegate lives but it is back from the beach.

This is clear but effective story-telling. Hemingway's technique appears uncomplicated, offering the reader a series of statements that build into a picture of the place and its history. There is, though, a skilful variation in the sentence length and rhythm, a variation that maintains interest. The only punctuation marks are the full stop and the comma, as if there is nothing here to question or excite. What we might also add is that the style is a loose sentence structure. The characteristic of loose sentences is that the main verb appears early and the qualifying or modifying phrases and clauses follow in succession, so that the effect is cumulative.

There is, of course, nothing loose about Hemingway's writing in the sense of words being wasted or unnecessary. 'Loose' or 'cumulative' is a rather old-fashioned term that modern linguists avoid but which is quite easy to remember to describe one kind of sentence structure. The sentence usually begins with the subject and verb and then adds more information. The opposite kind of sentence is the periodic sentence in which the main verb appears comparatively late; all or most of the qualifying or modifying clauses and phrases precede it, and consequently suspend the completion of the sense and construction until the end. This is from Dickens's *Great Expectations* at a point where the hero Pip, now an adult, sees Estella, his childhood sweetheart:

> But she was so much changed, was so much more beautiful, so much more womanly, in all things winning admiration had made such wonderful advance, that I seemed to have made none.

The effect of sentences such as this is to add weight to the end, or to build to a climax.

A third kind of sentence is known as the balanced sentence. This is made up of two main clauses that are closely similar in structure, as in John F. Kennedy's words:

> Let us never negotiate out of fear, but let us never fear to negotiate.

Or we can take this example from Jane Austen's *Emma*. Here the heroine is considering a proposal of marriage she has received:

> She thought nothing of his attachment, and was insulted by his hopes. He wanted to marry well, and having the arrogance to raise his eyes to her, pretended to be in love; but she was perfectly easy as to his not suffering any disappointment that need be cared for.

The point about balanced sentences is their symmetry and neatness of structure, features which lend an air of something being carefully thought out and weighed. For this reason, balanced sentences are favoured by politicians and speech-writers who want to make an emphatic but seemingly reasonable statement. They are, it has to be said, fairly rare in academic work, but you might spot one in your reading.

In your writing the chances are that most of your sentences will be of the loose kind. This is partly because loose sentences lend themselves very easily to revealing information in a direct way, whereas periodic sentences hold back and do not reveal the full force of what is being suggested until the end. It is for this reason that they can, occasionally, be very useful and very effective in argument. Everything in the end, however, depends on the situation and the type of work you are producing. In many cases a mixture of sentence types may be desirable: long and short, simple and complex, loose and periodic. The key thing is to be aware of what you are doing in your writing and why.

Too little, too much

There is, as we said at the start of this chapter, everything to be said for simple, well-constructed sentences. Some students, however, find it difficult to write any more than two or three sentences in a paragraph; they run out of ideas or they feel they have said everything they want to say. There is, of course, nothing to be gained by filling pages unnecessarily, and it is certainly not the case that the longest essays get the best marks. Nevertheless, there may be times when you are selling yourself short by not clarifying your points and rounding off your paragraphs. This is where loose sentences come into their own: they allow you to add to your argument with comparative ease simply because they are the kind of sentence that carry information or detail in a straightforward way.

Let's look at an example. This is from an essay about Anita Brookner's prize-winning novel *Hotel du Lac*, dealing with its representation of women. The novel tells the story of the aftermath of a failed love affair, with the heroine sent abroad to recover in an isolated hotel. In the first paragraph the student outlined the main issues in the question, and then in the next paragraphs began to build the answer in more detail. The second paragraph ran as follows:

> The novel's opening description focuses on the setting of the hotel among gloomy mountains and a rather depressing landscape. There is at first no sunlight or colour mentioned, and everything seems lifeless and dank. Brookner writes of how 'From the window all that could be seen was a receding area of grey', and how 'the grey garden' 'seemed to sprout nothing but the stiffish leaves of some unfamiliar plant'.

The paragraph starts usefully enough, but it doesn't arrive anywhere; the student has got so far with the analysis of the text, but then stopped short of pulling the points into the orbit of the question. What is needed is a final sentence that will explain the significance of what the writer has spotted so that we feel we have reached a conclusion. For example:

> The novel's opening description focuses on the setting of the hotel among gloomy mountains and a rather depressing landscape. There is at first no sunlight or colour mentioned, and everything seems lifeless and dank. Brookner writes of how 'From the window all that could be seen was a

receding area of grey', and how 'the grey garden' 'seemed to sprout nothing but the stiffish leaves of some unfamiliar plant'. In this way Brookner prepares the reader for the sombre world of the women in the novel while also creating a sense of the threat that surrounds them even in their hotel retreat.

The sentence we have added rounds off the paragraph by linking the analysis of the text to the question. The sentence itself follows a straightforward format and serves to spell things out for the reader. If you have difficulties in writing enough for an essay, look at the structure of your paragraphs. Make sure that they have a clear shape: a topic sentence that sets up the paragraph, then analysis of the text or detail, and finally a conclusion that arrives somewhere.

This might be a good point to add a word about the concluding paragraph of an essay. There is little to be gained in an essay by adding a conclusion that merely repeats all the points made in the body of the text. Nor is there much to be gained by writing something like 'In conclusion, therefore, I have argued . . .'. What you can aim for in the conclusion is a much more interesting but perhaps general statement, showing you are still thinking and can see the implications of the case you have made. Have a look at how some academic essays in your subject area end to see how they manage both their introductions and conclusions. Sometimes it is useful to spend time just quickly glancing at the beginnings and endings of academic articles rather than reading them for their ideas in order to build up your reserves of essay-writing experience.

A different kind of problem faces students who find it hard to stick to the word limit for essays. Usually they have too much material, perhaps as a result of having a large number of ideas they want to include, or because they cannot see how to cut their essays. Both of these difficulties can often be cured by thinking about the style of the essay. There are lots of writers who say that the secret of good prose is what you cut out. You might start with 5,000 words, but if you only have 2,500 words available then that inevitably improves the quality of what you have to say. It does so because in the process of revision you go through trying to make everything sharper and more to the point.

The way to do this is to have a checklist: is the overall structure of the essay tight enough? Have you got too many short paragraphs? Have you got too many long paragraphs? Are your sentences too long and convoluted? Have you got too many examples in each paragraph? Have you overloaded your sentences with information at the expense of your argument? Getting to know how you write will help you decide what to cut, but it will also help you develop and change your style so that you spend less time on excising material and more time on polishing your essay.

The main point we are concerned to get across here is that there is more than one stage involved in writing; there is drafting, then redrafting, then redrafting until the essay actually works. Of course, you cannot do that in exams, but the more work you have done on developing your writing skills during the course, the more confident your one-off drafts will be in an exam. So you write, and then you rewrite, even if your essay is exactly the right number of words. But some people might feel at a total loss as to what to do in this rewriting stage. Essentially, however, that is what we have been explaining in the course of this book. You look at each sentence and ask: 'Is this actually a sentence? Does it seem to read all right? Does it have a subject–verb–object? Have I spliced it with another sentence? Where I have made a sentence more complex, have I worked in the extra phrases and clauses in the right way, and signalled them to the reader through my use of punctuation? And, if I am satisfied with the construction of the sentences, and the punctuation, do I appear to have spelled the words correctly, and have I used the right words? And does the essay look polished and professional in terms of presentation?' Finally, read the essay out loud to yourself; that, perhaps, is the most important technique of all in becoming a better writer.

▶ **Conclusion**

There might seem to be an awful lot of things you have to do and check in writing an essay, but in the end there is far less effort involved if you are aware of the rules and conventions and how to shape your work. People who have never been taught how to swim properly thrash about, wasting energy, making very little progress. People who have been taught how to swim move elegantly through the water, making rapid progress. The time you spend learning the rules and conventions, and checking that your own work complies with the handful of rules and conventions, isn't wasted; it is an effort that will save you time, and get you a better degree or exam result, in the long run. The reasons for that are not hard to find. Good writing creates ideas; the way you construct and present your essays helps you explore those ideas further. Each sentence becomes a way of controlling and refining your material so that the reader comes to see the sort of effort you have made to be clear and to construct an essay that arrives somewhere interesting. With practice, writing stops being a chore and becomes a skill and then transforms into something like a pleasure. And when writing becomes a pleasure, when you can see what you are doing and why, then it also becomes a very powerful instrument with which to persuade, impress and communicate.

A Note on Grammar

By grammar we usually mean the conventional system of rules for putting words together in a sentence. It includes the idea of placing the words in a suitable order, giving them appropriate endings and linking them in a grammatical way. Traditional grammar books take many of their ideas from Latin grammar and apply them to English. Modern descriptive linguists point out, however, that Latin is a misleading model to use and that English works largely on the basis of word order rather than inflections or changes to the endings of words as in Latin or many European languages. The two approaches share some of the same vocabulary but put very different emphases on it. While traditionalists are interested in the rules, linguists are much more interested in the form and function of language.

We have outlined these two different approaches because you need to be aware of them when reading around. Perhaps the best modern approach is to be found in David Crystal's *Rediscover Grammar*; a more traditional approach, but one that is also helpful, is James R. Hurford's *Grammar. A Student's Guide*. We have also found Shirley Russell's *Grammar, Structure and Style* very useful. On punctuation, the most user-friendly work is R. L. Trask's *The Penguin Guide to Punctuation*; the handiest small reference book is *Chambers Good English Guide*, which again is very traditional.

But how much grammar do you really need to know in order to write well? The answer, as we suggested in the introduction, is very little, and we hope we have covered the three main areas in the body of the book. They are: (i) subject, verb and object; (ii) main clause and subordinate clause; (iii) simple sentence, compound sentence and complex sentence. If you know what these are, and also know how to punctuate, then you should be able to write an essay with few difficulties. You should also be able to make sense of and profit from the books listed above. They all deal with grammar in a practical, sensible way, which is the best way to tackle the topic.

All of us are, in fact, already experts in grammar by virtue of our ability to read, write, speak and think. Grammar books help us identify and understand these processes. Essentially there is nothing mysterious about grammar. Its terminology may not always be very attractive, but for the most part much of it is common sense. It is, though, important for students to know their way round the topic and to come to grips with it. The summaries that follow try to outline the basics.

▶ Grammar summary

1. A **simple sentence** consists of a single main clause.
2. A **compound sentence** consists of two or more simple sentences joined together by a co-ordinating conjunction such as *and* or *but* or *or*.
3. A **complex sentence** consists of one or more main clauses and one or more subordinate clauses.
4. The **subject** of a sentence occurs first in a statement or is what a sentence is about.
5. The **object** of a sentence is the person or thing on which the action of the main verb is performed.
6. The **main or finite verb** is a verb that is marked for tense and normally agrees with or matches its subject in person (e.g. *I*, *she*, *they*) and number (singular or plural). More simply, it is the ordinary use of the verb, not the infinitive (*to*) or participle (*-ing*) forms.
7. **Non-finite verb forms** are the infinitive or base form, the present participle and the past participle. These are non-finite forms of the verb because they do not show person, number or tense.
8. The **main or independent clause** is a group of words that contains a subject and a main verb: it is the main structure of the sentence and can stand on its own as a sentence.
9. The **subordinate or dependent clause** is a group of words that gives further information about the main clause. It may contain a finite or non-finite verb but cannot stand on its own as a sentence.
10. The **phrase** is a group of words that adds further information in the sentence. It does not contain a finite verb.
11. The **parts of speech** are nouns, pronouns, adjectives, verbs, adverbs, prepositions, conjunctions, the definite and indefinite articles (sometimes called determiners).
12. **Regular verbs** have four forms: the base form (*call*), the -s form (*calls*), the -ed form (*called*) and the -ing form (*calling*). English has two tenses: present (*call*) and past (*called*).
13. Other aspects of time are constructed using the **auxiliary verbs** *will*

and *shall*. Other auxilliary verbs are *to be*, *to have*, *may*, *might*, *would*, *should* and *must*. *Can* and *could* are also used as auxiliaries.

14. A **transitive verb** needs an object to make sense: *She closed the door*.

15. An **intransitive verb** does not take an object: *I awoke*; *the stranger listened greedily*. Other intransitive verbs include *sit* and *die*.

16. **Active and passive** Verbs can be used in two different ways: actively or passively. When the subject does the action, the verb is said to be in the 'active voice': *The child picked the flowers*. We can then turn this sentence round so that it becomes passive: *The flowers were picked by the child*. Here the verb *were picked* is in the passive voice. In the first sentence, *the flowers* are the object; in the second sentence, *the flowers* are the subject. They are not, however, the doer of the action but the recipient of it.

17. **Number**. 'Number' means singular or plural.

18. **Person**. 'Person' is a technical term indicating who is speaking, being spoken to or spoken about. The first-person singular is *I*, the first-person plural is *we*. The second-person is *you*; the third-person singular is *he* or *she* or *it*; the third-person plural is *they*.

19. **Sentences** are made up of clauses; there are just five **clause elements**: subject, verb, object, complement and adverbial. Thus:

    (S) The teacher / (V) has called / (O) me / (C) a genius / (A) several times.

20. Nearly all **clauses** follow the same pattern in which the subject (S) precedes the verb (V), and the verb (V) precedes the object. Most sentences also follow the pattern SVO.

▶ Parts of speech

The parts of speech are the eight (sometimes nine) terms or categories traditional grammarians use to describe words and their jobs. Every word belongs to one of these categories which can be subdivided further. Modern descriptive linguists prefer the term word-class which lends itself more readily to a range of languages.

1. **Nouns:** a noun is a word used to name; it names people, things, animals, ideas, emotions, states or qualities: *baby*, *Robert*, *car*, *hope*, *anger*.

2. **Pronouns:** a pronoun stands in place of a noun: *I*, *she*, *he*, *it*, *we*, *you*, *they*.
3. **Adjectives:** an adjective describes or qualifies a noun or pronoun: the *fast* car, the *barking* dog.
4. **Verbs:** a verb is a word that expresses an action or a physical or mental state: the man *shouted*, I *am*, you *wish*, people *feel*, they *seem*. We should note that there is also a category called auxiliary verbs: these are the verbs *to be*, *to have* and the verbs/words *shall*, *will*, *may*, *might*, *do*, *would*, *should* and *must*. Auxiliary verbs combine with other verbs.
5. **Adverbs:** an adverb modifies the meaning of other parts of speech (except nouns and pronouns), telling us how, when, where or why something happens. Many adverbs end in 'ly': *softly*, *easily*; but the following are also adverbs: *now*, *often*, *too*.
6. **Conjunctions:** a conjunction serves to join single words, phrases or sentences. There are two types:
    (i) co-ordinating conjunctions, which join two or more main clauses: *and*, *but*, *or*, *nor*, *for*, *so*, *yet*.
    (ii) subordinating conjunctions, which join a dependent or subordinate clause to a main clause: *after*, *although*, *as if*, *because*, *if*, *when*, *while*.
7. **Prepositions:** prepositions indicate spatial or temporal position: *on*, *to*, *up*, *between*, *over*.
8. **Articles:** the indefinite article is the word *a* (*an* before a vowel sound); the definite article is the word *the* and is used to refer to a specific thing or person, while the indefinite is used when no particular object is specified.

If you have managed to negotiate that mass of information, you will realise that, in a sense, we are back where we started at the beginning of this book: writing is a matter of the right words (and sometimes it is useful to know if a word is a noun, or a verb, etc.), and getting the right words in the right order, that is, making sure that your sentences correspond with the basic rules of grammar. Gaining command of these matters is no more difficult than learning to drive; it only seems more difficult because these few simple rules about sentence formation permit such an extraordinary number and permutation of possible sentences.

Twenty to Remember

Many of the difficulties over punctuation and grammar are caused by the use of the comma (,) and the apostrophe ('). This list is largely about how to use these. A tick (✓) means right; an asterisk (*) means something is technically wrong.

1. Avoid comma splices

* The French are good at cooking, the British are good at eating.

This is wrong because a comma cannot join two sentences. There are plenty of alternative ways to do this:

✓ The French are good at cooking, while the British are good at eating.

✓ The French are good at cooking, the British at eating.

✓ The French are good at cooking; the British are good at eating.

✓ The French are good at cooking, the British are good at eating, while the Italians are good at everything.

2. Avoid sentence fragments

* Many trees shed their leaves. Which happens in winter.

This is wrong because the fragment after the full stop is a subordinate clause and cannot stand on its own as a sentence. This can be corrected in several ways:

✓ Many trees shed their leaves, which happens in winter.

✓ Many trees shed their leaves, and this happens in winter.

✓ Many trees shed their leaves; this happens in winter.

✓ Many trees shed their leaves. This happens in winter.

3. Do not join sentences using 'however', 'therefore', 'yet', 'nevertheless'

> * The moon is bright tonight, however, tomorrow it will be dull.

This is wrong because sentences cannot be joined by these words following a comma. Use a semicolon or full stop instead:

> ✓ The moon is bright tonight; however, tomorrow it will be dull.

> ✓ The moon is bright tonight. However, tomorrow it will be dull.

4. Join sentences using 'and', 'or', 'but', 'yet' 'while'
The following are all correct:

> ✓ The moon is bright tonight, and it will stay bright tomorrow.

> ✓ The moon is bright tonight, but tomorrow it will be dull.

> ✓ The sea is calm tonight, yet it has rained all day.

> ✓ The car crashed there, or it may have been here.

> ✓ The British are good at eating, while the French are good at drinking.

5. Making a list

> * We drink French, red wine a lot.

This is wrong because you cannot substitute the word **and** for the comma here. This is the test for listing commas:

> ✓ We drink French red wine a lot.

> ✓ My favourite novelists are Austen, Eliot, Lawrence and Joyce.

> ✓ His long, dark, bushy beard appeared silly.

6. Commas in pairs

> * She looked for her keys, and finding them, quickly drove off.

This is wrong because if you take out the words between the commas the sentence no longer makes sense. This is the essential test for bracketing commas:

> ✓ She looked for her keys and, finding them, quickly drove off.

> * Morrison's *The Bluest Eye* published in 1970, was her first novel.

This second example is wrong because there is only one comma:

✓ Morrison's *The Bluest Eye*, published in 1970, was her first novel.

7. Proper names and clauses

* Kate James who is now a judge went to a comprehensive school.

This is wrong because the clause here does not add essential information and so commas are needed:

✓ Kate James, who is now a judge, went to a comprehensive school.

8. The words 'although', 'though', 'even though', 'because', 'since', 'after', 'before', 'if', 'when' and 'whenever' and the beginning of sentences

Where these are part of a long introduction to a main sentence, divide them off by a comma:

✓ Before the war of 1914 and the coming of hard austerity measures, they lived a pleasant life.

With shorter phrases the comma is not essential, but can be included:

✓ Before the war in 1914 they lived a pleasant life.

✓ Before the war in 1914, they lived a pleasant life.

9. The end of sentences – the full stop

It might seem too obvious to state, but you need a full stop at the end of a sentence.

✓ I think this is pretty fair, all things considered.

✓ I think, all things considered, this is pretty fair.

10. The semicolon

The semicolon can always be replaced by a full stop but not by a comma:

* She was the best of friends, she was the worst of enemies.

This is wrong because a comma cannot join two sentences:

✓ She was the best of friends; she was the worst of enemies.

✓ She was the best of friends. She was the worst of enemies.

11. The colon

Most commonly, the colon precedes a kind of clarifying definition, or introduces a list:

✓ Britain is facing a huge problem: no one can spell.

✓ Several people turned up: the butcher, the baker and the candle-stick maker.

12. Use a semicolon when joining sentences with 'however', 'therefore', 'hence', 'nevertheless', 'meanwhile' and 'consequently'

* The house caught fire, however, the paintings were saved.

This is a comma splice and so is wrong. All the above words – that is, **however, therefore, hence, nevertheless, meanwhile** and **consequently** – require a semicolon before them when they are used to join two sentences together:

✓ The house caught fire; however, the paintings were saved.

This could also be turned into two sentences:

✓ The house caught fire. However, the paintings were saved.

The same example:

* The house caught fire, nevertheless, the paintings were saved.

✓ The house caught fire; nevertheless, the paintings were saved.

A final example:

* The house caught fire, consequently, the paintings were destroyed.

✓ The house caught fire; consequently, the paintings were destroyed.

13. The apostrophe and plural nouns

The apostrophe does not make words plural:

* Car's for sale; video's here.

The first of these means the 'car is for sale'; the second one means the 'video is here'. The plural is simply as follows:

✓ Cars for sale; videos here; pizzas delivered; bikes sold; new potatoes.

14. Apostrophe s: the possessive

✓ Jane's dog; children's clothes; time's winged chariot; James's book.

The trick here is to add 'apostrophe s' to the word, which must be a real English word as it is normally spelt: *Jane*, *children*, *time*, *James*.

15. Plural nouns ending in s and the apostrophe: the possessive

✓ the girls' books; two days' time; the Joneses' car (that is, the car belonging to the Joneses, the plural of Jones)

The trick is to add just an apostrophe to the plural word, which must be a real plural word. So, *ladie's hats* is wrong, but *ladies' hats* is right; *mens' socks* is wrong, but *men's socks* is right.

16. Personal pronouns do not have apostrophe s

* It is mine'; it is your's; it is her's; it is his'; it is their's; it is ours'; it is it's house.

These are all wrong because the words *mine*, *yours*, *hers*, *his*, *theirs*, *ours* and *its* are already possessives:

✓ It is mine; it is yours; it is hers; it is his; it is theirs; it is ours; it is its house.

17. It's and its

It's means it is or it has.

✓ It's raining.

This is right: it means 'It is raining'.

✓ It's been raining

This is right: it means 'It has been raining'.

Remind yourself that apostrophe 's' in *it's* is a verb.

Its means belonging to it

✓ The dog wagged its tail.

This is right.

Remind yourself that 'its' is like the word 'bits': the bits of a dog are its tail, its ears and its legs.

18. Speech marks and punctuation

✓ "I am," he said, "a lost soul."

✓ "That's enough," barked the captain. "We must be brave."

Different publishers have different conventions (some use single quotation marks); the only rule is be consistent.

If you are quoting from a text, remember to indent (without quotation marks) any extract of three or more lines.

19. Hyphen

✓ It is the twentieth century.

✓ It is a twentieth-century design.

But note we write *the swiftly moving car*, not *swiftly-moving*.

20. The correct word

✓ The house is over there.

✓ It is their house.

✓ That should not affect the result.

✓ The effect was felt far and wide.

✓ The principal dancer was Russian.

✓ The principle has been adopted by all parties.

If you can see why these are right or wrong, then you should have no difficulty at all with writing an essay or with communicating your ideas in a clear and precise fashion. The list is intended to remind you to check everything you write to make sure that it is easy to read and says what you want it to say. In the end, that is why we write and why we need to know about writing.